The story of abuse is never an eas
and hearts bruised and battered. 1
must-read for all of us who think,
world'. *A Life Unimagined* not only tells the truth boldly and openly,
but also shines a ray of hope for those who may still feel trapped in the
lonely and fearful world of the abused.

—*Pastor Peter Tate, former Pastor of Marton Assembly of God,*
Professional Supervisor and Consultant

Looking from the outside at someone else's life, you may see the ups
and downs, the good times and the bad, but it is nowhere near the
same as being that person who is living that life.

I was a spectator looking in on Keren's life. I saw her good times
and some of the results of the bad. I was able to see some of the wins
and losses, but I never knew the turmoil, suffering and pain that was
Keren's life before Heaven interrupted the negative spiral, the darkness,
the pain and heartache.

Having known Keren as a young girl, and watching as her life
seemed to go from one deep pit to the next, it is truly awesome to
now see her as a completely different person. Keren's life story is living
proof that there is always hope; that try as we may, there is no denying
the wonders that happen when God is allowed into a person's life.

This gritty, frank and often gut-wrenching story shows that no
matter how deep in the pit a person may be, and despite how bad and
desperate a situation may be, there is a Father who is willing to take us
at our most broken and lovingly put the pieces back together.

This account of Keren's life is a testament to her passion to never
give up, to never say die, to hold onto hope, and to believe in a God
who is faithful, who will do amazing things, turning suffering, pain
and despair into joy, wholeness and hope.

—*Pastor Phil Dent*

Having known Keren as a happy, cheerful, content child, it came as a shock to read about the breakaway from her family due to a controlling and abusive relationship.

As I read how she was able to break out of the prison she was in, I found myself thinking that Keren's writing of this book has been part of the healing process for her, and it will be a tremendous help to others who have been through traumatic life experiences.

—*Pastor Ann Perry*

I count it an honour to have Keren ask me to write this endorsement for her book. My relationship with the Maas family began in 1980 shortly after Keren was born. I was the pastor of her family church in Marton. The Maas's were an example of what Christian family represented— caring, loving, a fun-filled home, and two parents happily married and committed to build a healthy and stable family. My wife and I knew Keren's mum and dad well and would often visit the family farm.

Having read Keren's book, *A Life Unimagined*, I applaud her for her transparency and honesty in presenting her story. How sad and yet how common Keren's story is, repeated over and over again in many families. I endorse the accuracy from being the family's pastor from 1980-1988. I watched on from 1988 from a distance to see the broken hearts of a mother and father as the lives of their children unravelled over the following years. I read with great joy that Keren returned to her faith and began to sort her life out.

Keren, I endorse your book, and my hope is that it will provide a fence at the top of the cliff and prevent families from the hurt and damage that you have experienced. Well done.

—*Pastor Denis Humphreys*

We all have a story, things from our past that have moulded us and shaped us through life's journey. Many stories remain untold, hidden in the recesses of the past, so I am thrilled that Keren has had the courage to tell her story.

This book is not written out of a need to be 'heard', but from Keren's heart that is genuine and honest. When one's soul is broken, dreams are shattered and hope is lost in physical and mental exhaustion, restoration can seem out of reach. By writing her story Keren seeks to help those who have also gone through abusive relationships to restore their trust in others, have a hope for the future, to have faith in God, and to learn to love oneself again.

—Lilias McMinn Collard,
Mentor and friend

If you are unsure whether God will accept you or relate with you because you feel you are not good enough, this book is a must-read. We have known Keren for many years and we have found her to be honest, upright and transparent. This is a story about God's faithfulness. Keren's life story is full of many ups and downs. On multiple occasions, she hit rock bottom, and it felt like she may not come through, but God always came through. He never abandoned her, but pursued her with love.

—Pastors Jessy and Sajan Easow,
Revived and Restored Ministries

A LIFE UNIMAGINED

Torn Curtain Publishing
Wellington, New Zealand
www.torncurtainpublishing.com

ISBN Softcover 978-0-473-63458-2

Cataloguing in Publishing Data
    Title: A Life Unimagined
    Author: Keren Maas
    Subjects: Personal memoir, Christian life, Spirituality, Relationships, Abuse and recovery

A copy of this book is held at the National Library of New Zealand

A LIFE UNIMAGINED

My Journey from Abuse
to Redemption

Keren Maas

Dedication

To family who have gone before me. Thank you for your Godly lives and the legacy of faith you have passed down through the generations. I pray that I can continue to pass the legacy on to those to come.

To Mum and Dad. Thank you for giving me a wonderful childhood filled with so many cherished memories. Thank you for your unconditional love, and for never, ever giving up on me.

To my beautiful daughters, Janaya, Sanjanah and Ahnaliyah. You are my absolute pride and joy. You represent the very best parts of me. I am so proud to be your mum and to see the amazing women you have become. My love for you is immeasurable.

To my precious grandchildren, Cassius and Evei-Manea, my little prince and princess. Mema loves you forever and always.

To my future grandchildren, and all the generations to come. Although you are yet to be conceived and born, I love you dearly already. I pray God would make Himself known to you, and that you would live your lives loving and honouring Him, just as your forefathers have done.

To my readers who have experienced hurt and abuse, or who struggle with addiction, depression or suicidal thoughts. I pray my story gives you hope that things can get better. Please never give up.

From the Author's Children

Dear Mum,

When I read your original (much-shorter) testimony years ago it gave me a small insight into the trials you faced in your younger years. Years later, and after having moved out of home and had my own life experiences, I understand your struggles and pain so much more than I did as a child.

I am so excited to read your book and to learn even more of your journey and to be encouraged and inspired by your strength and resilience. I know that many others will also be moved and inspired by your story too.

Like you, I became a young mum. You and I went through similar experiences at similar ages with relationships and teenage motherhood. I understand now, Mum, and I want to say thank you for all you've done and for never giving up. Thank you for raising me and my sisters single-handedly, and thank you for loving us and always doing your best. I know it was a struggle at times, and although times were often tough we never went without. You always found a way to provide for us and to give us fun experiences.

You deserve so much more than the world ever offered you.

—Janaya

Dear Mum,

I know we didn't always have it easy growing up and I couldn't imagine raising three daughters on your own but you did it, and you did it with nothing short of constant love. Despite everything that was thrown against you, every day you showed me the strength you had. You've taught me that I can face any challenge that gets in my way. If I grow up to be half the kind of mum you are then I know that I'm doing good. I'm so proud that you're sharing your story and I know that it will reach many. I don't say this enough but I love you and thank you for everything you have done for me and continuously do.

—Sanjanah

Dear Mum,

I'm proud of how you've stayed resilient through all the challenges you have faced and how you have only done your best to provide for us girls. We know you never intended to raise us on your own. Although we don't say it enough we are very grateful for all you do and the sacrifices you've made to make it to where you are.

—Ahnaliyah

Foreword

It is a real privilege to write this foreword for Keren Maas who, along with her girls, I have known for over ten years now, most of that time as their pastor.

A pastor's role is unique and privileged in ways many other roles would struggle to match. You have a front seat to both the greatest depth of challenges and heights of celebrations, and find yourself in rooms you would have no place being in otherwise.

While much of Keren's story predates my time, there have certainly been many seasons where I've seen her navigate these challenges in person rather than through words on a page.

I was so moved by Keren's vulnerability and bravery telling her story. Keren's story highlights the faithfulness of God and His unending love for His children. It resonates authentically with me, and I pray Keren's journey would be the very hope that is required for others facing similar challenges and disappointments.

Thank you, Keren, for your obedience in sharing your journey. You've created something here to be really proud of.

—Ps. Peter Brothers
Equippers Church Hastings

This book contains graphic accounts of the author's personal experience, including child endangerment, domestic violence, sexual and physical assault and drug use. This story is not intended to be read by minors.

Contents

A Legacy of Faith

The Maas family legacy is steeped in faith. The following letter, entitled 'Last Words to my Dear Family', was written more than a century ago by my great-great-great-grandfather in Bassum, Germany.

February 1880

My dearly beloved Children!

When Almighty God decrees that I leave this world, harken to my last words, and may they always be remembered by you all. I have provided for your earthly needs, and if you are wise and thrifty you should suffer no want, but remember always that without Godliness and goodness no true happiness is possible on this earth.

Hold fast to God's Word. It is surely your greatest happiness, both in this world and the next. May you always value your faith as precious and holy; then the thought of God and your life's end should never trouble you or cause you any fear.

Never close your hearts to those who suffer or who are poor, but always be ready to help. Be conscientiously faithful and honest; remember always that it is better to suffer wrong than to do wrong. Love your enemies, and never return hatred with hatred. Guard against gambling and drunkenness, and be complete master over your will and desires.

Above all, flee from the sinful desires of the flesh which poison both body and soul. Beware of greed, the root of all evil, which can easily be mistaken for wise thriftiness. And should you in due course become your own master and employer of labour, be kind and thoughtful to those who work for you, and to your fellow men. Honour your superiors, and always obey the laws of the land.

My children, love one another sincerely, and should one of you suffer need, let the others give help, even if it means sacrificing your possessions.

I know that your teachers have already taught you all I have written here; I only wish to tell you that these have always been the guiding principles of my life, and doubtless will become yours as well.

And so farewell, my dear children. May God the Father guide you through this life and keep you all in times of suffering and temptation. Place your complete trust in the assurance that God's ways are always best for us. For when I look back on my life, I can only thank God for His many blessings and say, "Father You have truly done all things well." Remember often, your father will love you eternally.

Dear God, source of all true happiness, I commend to you in firm confidence, all my dear children. Be a loving father to them as you have been to me.

To this day, copies of this letter take pride of place in the homes of many of my extended family members, even those who are not walking with the Lord. It is beautiful to see these wise words being kept and treasured throughout the generations. How grateful I am today for the faith of those who have gone before me. God honours that faith, and although our stories take many difficult turns, He remains faithful to rescue, restore and redeem families for His glory.

Preface

I entered the world in the spring of 1980 at the Marton maternity home in New Zealand. I was three weeks premature. The number one song in New Zealand on the day I was born was *Food for Thought* by UB40 and Robert Muldoon was the Prime Minister. I spent my first four days in an incubator, fed through a tube.

Mum and Dad took turns naming their children. It was Dad's turn when it came to naming me, the fourth of four girls. It took him over ten days but eventually I was named Keren after the biblical prophet Job's youngest daughter, Keren-Happuch. Keren is a Hebrew name meaning 'ray of light'.

From a young age I dreamed of falling in love, getting married and having a family of my own. I had no idea of the abuse, pain and heartache that was to come.

This is my story . . .

"You have taken note of my journey through life, caught each of my tears in your bottle."

Psalm 56:8, TV

1

The Magic of Innocence

Rays of incandescent sunlight filtered through the entanglement of reeds that framed the tunnel. I gazed into the hollow, my heart pounding triple time with unbridled excitement as I marvelled at the glowing light that emanated from the other side. I looked up at my dad, and with breathless anticipation asked, "Is this the way to Heaven?"

I cannot recall how my dad responded. I'm positive, however, that his answer would have been characteristically creative, preserving the magic of my imagination as always. I do know that from that day on, the concrete pipe underneath the road became my favourite spot on our family farm. My dad and I would sometimes crawl inside to have picnics. To this day I fondly refer to it as 'Heaven', not so much because of the special times we had there, but because it reminds me of those who describe their near-death experience as 'a tunnel with light at the end'.

My childhood growing up on a farm evokes nostalgic and cherished memories of loving parents and simpler times. It was truly paradise at 'Little Urara'. Our white stucco house with its red tin roof, was encircled by a verdant fenced-off garden with an array of forget-me-nots, geraniums, cinerarias, irises, polyanthus and pansies in a myriad of colours. A vibrant growth of purple and white agapanthus lined the gravel driveway, and a beautiful, sweet-smelling clematis vine with pale pink flowers grew over the front fence. A camellia tree boasted beautiful crimson blossoms, and the pohutukawa bushes were adorned with a brilliant display of striking red blooms in summer.

To reach our house, you opened a moss-mottled, rickety old wooden gate tied shut with a loop of baling twine hooked over a round wooden fencepost. A spindly kowhai tree sat in the middle of the lawn just inside the gate. We called it the 'caterpillar tree' as it was often overrun with small, orange-headed green caterpillars. We also grew plums, apples, feijoa and rhubarb.

The house itself was 'retro', much like all the other homes of that era. I remember the 60's-style wallpaper with its flowery motifs and circle patterns, considered so fashionable at the time! Our television was small and box-like with large antennae, and it sat on a shelf in the kitchen. When I was very small, Mum did all the cooking on a coal range. Later, this was replaced with a pot-bellied stove. At night, with the lights off, I loved to see the chimney glowing red-hot from the heat that stove put out.

Our home had four bedrooms, and I have vague memories of sharing a room with my sister Ingrid. We swapped rooms from time to time and that was always fun, rearranging the furniture and settling into a new space. My favourite room had pink curtains and more of that wonderful retro wallpaper in a floral pattern of pastel pink, blue and green.

* * *

Our farm consisted of one-hundred-and-twenty acres of fine land situated outside a small country town in the North Island of New

Zealand. For my sisters and I, it was our own private playground.

We gave each of the paddocks on 'Little Urara' a name: Home Paddock, Front Paddock, Back Paddock, Round Paddock, Hayshed Paddock, and the Cabbage Tree Paddock (although as often as I looked, I never did see any cabbages growing on those cabbage trees!). The 'home paddock' was near the house outside the garden fence. It was there that I learned to ride a motorbike, doing circuits around the perimeter in first gear because I didn't know how to change to second. We also had box targets in the home paddock, which we shot at with bows and arrows. Sometimes, my dad hooked my kite to his fishing line, and as the unlocked reel spun, the line would grow longer and longer as the wind pulled the kite high into the sky. It was the perfect environment for a carefree upbringing rich in imagination.

* * *

"Dad, can we dig up the home paddock and make it into a big pool to keep pet dolphins in?" I asked. I was around six years old, and dreamed of transforming the grassy paddock outside our kitchen window into a crystal-clear pool. It was my backyard utopia, set against the breath-taking backdrop of Mount Ruapehu to the north and the majestic Mount Taranaki to the west. My mind conjured up images of dolphins swimming gracefully through the glistening water, leaping high in the air as they frolicked and played. I imagined the dolphins darting towards me when I ventured to the water's edge so I could jump in and give them cuddles. They would reciprocate with enthusiasm, letting me hold their dorsal fins while they pulled me playfully through the water.

My dad's reply to my fanciful petition would most likely have been, "We'll have to see about that." This was one of his most common responses to any request that warranted a yes or no answer. As his children grew older, however, this response became less of an optimistic acknowledgement and more a frustratingly inconclusive non-answer.

My dolphin fantasy epitomised the pure, untainted innocence of my childhood, a time when my creativity and dreams knew no limit. As it should be in childhood, my enchanted imaginings were not hindered by the constraints of adult realities. I believed in Father Christmas, the Easter Bunny and the Tooth Fairy. Classic family movies fed my wild imagination with abundance: Walt Disney's *Swiss Family Robinson* had me daydreaming about living in a tree house, and after seeing *Born Free* I yearned for adventures on an African safari. Every day seemed like a magical adventure of endless possibilities.

I often played with my cousin David, or friends from church. One of our favourite places was 'The Hill', where the towering pines grew. Together we would collect pine cones for the fire, scampering about in the logs and lush undergrowth, playing hide and seek and having adventures in an old rusted-out blue truck called Majesty. We made daisy-chains, plucked the petals from red clover flowers to suck out the sweetness, held buttercups under our chins to see if we liked butter, blew dandelion seeds to watch them float through the air like fairies, and hunted for cicada shells in the garden.

We built huts out of tangled vines and brushwood, played in the creek, got lost in the cornfields, climbed trees, and made toast on the burning grass at the edge of the paddock while Dad did burn-offs. Magpies swooped and chased us as we rode our pushbikes, my legs turning to jelly and my heart pounding out of my chest as I pedalled as fast as I could to get away.

The farm was home not only to the sheep and cows we raised, but also to a menagerie of other animals we adored and cared for, including a goat who loved to eat carrots and would tip his head back as he chewed as if sculling a drink from a bottle. I named him Sonny Spoon after a TV character. Then there were the horses, and a black sheep dog named Midnight, who Mum recalls was "not any help at all" on the farm. My sister Brigitta kept an adorable baby possum in one of Dad's old, woollen socks, and to this day we all share delightful memories of our beloved pet sheep Fat Lamb, who ate Weet-Bix out of our hands and danced and hopped around the campfire with great excitement while Dad sang and played his guitar.

Stray felines found their way to our farm in droves. Our cats must have been very welcoming because, much to my delight, we constantly discovered new litters of kittens.

Adventures extended beyond our farm, however. My imagination knew no bounds, especially when we set off for an outing at Santoft Beach. The ride through forestry land to and from the beach was a bumpy one, and I would stare out the car window scanning for bears and exotic wildlife amongst the trees. Once we arrived, I'd stand at the top of the black sand dunes which seemed massive to me, dizzyingly high and steep. Looking down the slopes, I was almost too afraid to slide down on the woven plastic barley sacks we brought along to use as sleds.

Santoft Beach is still known for a shipwrecked barge called the *Fusilier,* which ran ashore in January 1884 and was used as target practice by training pilots during World War II. The *Fusilier* has now been swallowed up into the sand dunes, but when I was a child, parts of it were clearly visible, poking out of the sand. This giant, weathered ship resting in the sand seemed magical to me as a child, and I envisioned a hoard of treasure concealed within, chests bursting with gold and precious jewels.

At home, I wrote letters to members of the Royal Family—one to Queen Elizabeth, another to Lady Diana, and one to Princess 'Fergie'. My excitement was immense when I received letters back! I knew these replies were from their Ladies-in-Waiting, but I imagined these royal 'helpers' writing back to me while sitting in grand chairs covered in luxurious red velvet at stately, dark-stained tables with intricate detailing, inside an enchanted castle built of large grey rugged bricks, with spiral stone staircases, towering turrets, and a gigantic wooden drawbridge across a moat filled with snapping crocodiles. My whole world was full of magic and adventure! One day, I thought, I would explore these foreign places for myself. Just like the children in *The Adventures of the Wishing Chair* and *The Folk of the Faraway Tree*, marvellous adventures in all sorts of wonderful lands awaited me.

* * *

My parents were practical, hardworking people, with broad smiles and a love of the farming life. Dad was rarely seen without a trucker's hat, his dark brown hair dishevelled beneath it, except when he was going to church, when he would comb it into place with Brylcreem. Dad wore a full beard. It was his trademark, and I still remember the day he shaved it off. I was so shocked when I saw him emerge from the bathroom that I didn't know whether to laugh or cry because he looked so different!

Dad was a farming contractor and also a respected elder in the Assemblies of God church in Marton. Other church families regularly visited our home for meals, fellowship and prayer, as well as noisy card games that caused uncontrollable laughter. The youth group would often come out to our farm as well, to play spotlight at night.

Peter Tate, a former pastor of the church in Marton, remembers those early youth group days. "We all enjoyed being invited out to the farm," he said. "Kay was an excellent hostess and fed us very well. She always had a yummy spread set out for us. She tolerated the noisy invasions with huge quantities of grace. Lindsay was a very kind and thoughtful man. He was a deep thinker and thought through every decision carefully. I used to love talking with him."

Likewise, Denis Humphreys, another pastor, has fond memories. "Lindsay was a faithful man," he recalls. "He was an Elder in the Marton church with me. He gave me great support and was always available in times of need. I spent many times at the farm with Kay and Lindsay. We worked together and milled the farm's old shelter belt (row of trees planted as a windbreak). Lindsay was a generous man, devoted to his wife and family."

As well as church friends calling in, it was not uncommon to have strangers turn up at our door. I knew there was something special about my home, because sometimes people would arrive saying they had been driving past on the highway and God had spoken to them. He had told them that our house was one where God was worshiped and they could stop in for prayer. At the time, it seemed quite normal to me.

As a child, I was intrigued by the thought of missionaries in far-off places. Mum and Dad supported a family of missionaries in India, and often wrote letters to them. I was intrigued by their daughter's name, Goldimere. I thought she must be a mermaid because 'Goldimere' sounded like the sort of name a mermaid might have!

My dad loved to play his guitar and I fondly remember him singing songs like: *Jesus, Sweet Jesus, Jesus Bids us Shine,* and *Jesus Loves Me.* He also sang songs such as *Purple People-Eater, How Much is that Doggy in the Window?, On Top of Spaghetti,* and *You are my Sunshine.*

My dad sang one song in particular, *The Railroad Goes Through the Middle of the House,* which caused me to picture the story in immense detail. I imagined a man in an old-style brown suit carrying a leather suitcase, knocking on the door of a rundown wooden house with chipped paint and overgrown grass protruding from underneath. Dad would give two knocks on the body of his guitar to add extra animation to the song, and as he did, I could visualise the bill collector in the lyrics coming inside, sitting on a wooden stool on the railway tracks that went right through the house, and drinking a cup of tea. I never put two and two together though, about why the people 'saw him no more'. Another favourite song Dad sang was called, *Ninety Miles an Hour.* I would giggle at the lyrics and beg Dad to sing it again and again!

Dad woke me up every morning by flinging open my bedroom curtains and singing, "Good morning, good morning, it is a lovely day!" and at night he would read to me from the Bible and pray with me, giving thanks and asking specifically for the things we had talked about. He always finished by laying his hand on my head and praying the words of Numbers 6:24-26: "The Lord bless you and keep you, Keren. The Lord make His face shine upon you, and be gracious to you; The Lord lift up His countenance upon you, and give you peace" (NKJV). Then he would tuck me in, tipping my mattress almost vertically, making me giggle as I was almost flipped off the other side.

Through the day, I helped Dad on the farm. Perched on his knee as he operated the open-cab harvester, I felt so high up, almost to the sky! It was like I was on top of the world looking down on the rotating spikes below us. As I grew older, I helped draft the sheep, marking their wool with chalk of different colours, and opening and closing the gates as Dad called out which paddock the sheep needed to go into. Most of all, I enjoyed riding on the motorbike with him in the early mornings or late evenings, then rushing inside to warm my freezing hands by the small bar-heater.

Lambing season was one of my favourite times on the farm. The spring air was crisp as I rode with Dad on the motorbike, checking on the ewes. I loved helping the ewes when they were having trouble, by pulling the lamb out. I can still smell the sanitiser Dad poured over my hands as I worked! He would find the legs, line them up for me, then I'd slip my hands in, get a firm grip on the legs, and pull. The sight of a new-born lamb always took my breath away. I was awed by the miracle of new life. The lambs came out yellow and the mother would instinctively lick her baby clean. I giggled as I watched the lambs wobble and fall as they learned to stand, their tails wriggling like crazy as they drank from their mother. You can't help but feel happy as you watch lambs frolicking and playing together. They look so animated and joyful, adorably tiny and brand new. Sadly, sometimes ewes passed away during birth and if this happened, we would bring the lambs into the house to keep them warm by the fire. I loved to cuddle them and feed them bottles of milk.

We also farmed cows, and a highlight was driving the tractor while Dad stood on the scoop at the back, throwing hay out to the cows. I couldn't reach the foot pedals, so Dad made a contraption to hold the accelerator down just a little. He told me to steer towards the sun, an instruction I took very seriously. I fixed my eyes firmly on the setting sun, constantly readjusting the steering wheel in tiny increments from left to right. Other times, we made trips together in the truck to drop off loads of grain at the silos in town.

Dad could fix anything and was always building or inventing things in his workshop. I liked being there too, and once we made a little wooden truck together. I slept with that truck every night for weeks because I loved it so much.

Often, we went fishing at the beach or the river, and Dad would read to me as we waited for fish to bite. I remember him reading Kathryn Kuhlman's *I Believe in Miracles,* the story of Gladys Aylward, and Douglas Lockwood's *Life on the Daly River.* Other times, we had picnics on the roof of the house, or slept on the back of the truck all night, gazing up at stars in a velvet black sky, spotting satellites and shooting stars.

As a family, we went to revival meetings in a big tent in the middle of town. Dad wore his orangey-brown suede jacket with wool inside. I remember cuddling up on his knee and falling asleep.

My dad had a great sense of humour and a contagious laugh. I remember hearing him from my bedroom, as he sat in the kitchen of an evening, watching television. He was a child at heart, cheeky and fun. He used to drive around and around roundabouts. Mum would give him a look after several loops and say, "Okay, that's enough now," and he'd turn around and smirk at us girls and do one more cheeky circuit. During outings to town, he would hop-scotch down the brick footpath.

At home, Dad was the same—full of fun and banter. He used to answer the phone by saying, "Chinese Railway Station, how can I help you?" People who knew Dad would just laugh and carry on, but those who didn't know him so well were often thrown by this unexpected greeting, and stumbled over their words, unsure how to respond. Whenever my mum asked Dad to do something around the house, he would say, "Yes, Bwana," a Swahili phrase which translates to "Yes, Master" or "Yes, Boss" which he'd picked up from a movie he'd watched.

* * *

Mum had short, wavy hair and a welcoming smile. She helped Dad on the farm when needed, drafting sheep and checking the cattle when he was away contracting. I remember picking swedes in the back paddock and sitting on the concrete steps of our enclosed porch helping Mum husk corn.

She was a terrific cook and baker, known far and wide for her wonderful food, and when it was time for tea, her voice carried all the way to the back of the farm. "Yoou hooo!" she called with an amazing ability, ensuring Dad knew it was time to finish up work and my sisters to come in from riding their horses.

We had pudding every night, and there was always baking in the house. If we happened to mention we felt like cake, Mum would get up and have started on it before the words even left our lips. Roasts and chocolate fudge were firm favourites. I worked right alongside Mum while she cooked, making mixtures with random ingredients like flour, chicken stock, sugar, tomato sauce, milk . . . whatever I could find. Everything went into a large bowl, mixed together. Delicious!

On the farm we sometimes hired young men to help at harvest time, and of course the shearing gangs visited regularly. Mum baked up a storm for these working gangs, and we carried loads of goodies over to the woolshed for the shearers to eat.

Mum loved music and could often be heard singing along with Kenny Rogers, BJ Thomas, Johnny Chester, and Elvis as she stewed apples and preserved jars of apricots, peaches, nectarines and plums.

As I grew older, I helped her cut up the fruit ready to be cooked.

There was always home-made ginger beer. Opening the bottles was nerve-wracking. We never knew if we'd hear a gentle hissing, or if there would be an explosion spraying the sticky sweet drink everywhere. As a toddler, if I was thirsty, I'd exclaim loudly, "I want a beer!" In fact, there is an often-told family story of how I yelled this out one day in church.

Mum made our clothes, sewing pyjamas and tracksuits, and knitting slippers. In several primary school photos, I can be seen in the front row wearing homemade tracksuits and gumboots, the epitome of style.

Like most kids, I watched a lot of television. Sunday nights were *MacGyver* nights. Mum and I would climb into her and Dad's bed to watch it, waiting for Dad to return from church with yummy treats that he'd buy from the petrol station on the way home.

One of Mum's most treasured possessions was a china cabinet her parents had bought her when she was sixteen. The cabinet displayed an array of ornaments, trinkets and knick-knacks, some of which were engagement and wedding presents, or birthday, Christmas and Mother's Day gifts from us girls. A special cup and saucer held pride of place in the cabinet. It had once belonged to Mum's Aunty Dolly who had received it when she was a toddler. Sadly, Aunty Dolly died in 1915 at the tender age of three, and my great-grandfather, Justus Ruhle, left this treasured set to Mum. She still has it to this day.

The excitement of Christmas was magical. I believed in Father Christmas, but I also knew Mum and Dad bought us presents as well. I remember my determination to find out where Mum hid those presents and my despair when that sacred hiding place eluded me. When we begged to be told what we were getting for Christmas, we'd be told, "A wigwam for a goose's bridle." It was a puzzling answer but one that spurred my imagination.

Mum pulled out all the stops at Christmas. I'd walk in the front door after school to be greeted by the heavenly aroma of Christmas cake baking in the oven, and the tangy pine scent of a real Christmas tree. A fabric advent calendar hung on the cupboard door. The twelve pockets had a treat for each of the twelve mornings leading up to Christmas day, often homemade baking wrapped in red or green cellophane.

On Christmas morning we woke to find stockings at the foot of our beds filled with fresh summer fruits and special treats. When I was very small, I'd wake up every Christmas morning, inspect the delicious stocking contents, then peer out the window hoping to see snow. I did not understand why it was always snowing on Christmas day in the movies but it never snowed at our house in New Zealand.

Christmas was a huge family occasion with Grandma and Grandad Maas and all our cousins, aunties and uncles. Grandma would do quizzes with us kids up in her bedroom at her house, handing out Mackintosh sweets as prizes.

Easter was another special time for our family. I have heart-warming memories of making chocolates in clear plastic moulds with Mum. Using a paint brush, we would spread the melted chocolate into the detailed moulds. Once set, we popped them out of the trays one by one and admired the different-shaped treats.

* * *

I have very few clear memories of my older sisters Melissa and Brigitta living at home. Perhaps, out of their immense love and their desire to protect and preserve our innocence, my parents sheltered us too much. As my sisters and I got older, we became intrigued with the enticing world that existed outside of the sanctuary of our home. Other teenagers spent their weekends partying, and were exploring the 'outside world'. Their lives were a mystery to us; most of our lives revolved around Christian friends and activities. Eventually, my older sisters pulled away from the world they knew, and became immersed in a life that broke my parents' hearts.

My sisters were sixteen and fourteen when they ran away from home. I remember that night with such clarity. The conversation around the dinner table that night left Dad feeling helpless and distraught about the direction his daughters' lives were taking. Out of sheer frustration he thumped his fist down on the kitchen table where we were all sitting, and my bowl of ice cream and blueberries from Grandad's berry patch went flying off the table and onto the floor. I watched it fall as if in slow motion, then burst into tears over my spoiled dessert while my sisters took off outside. My memories are hazy after that, but Melissa and Brigitta left that night and began their 'grown up' lives.

I became an aunty at the age of six when Melissa gave birth to her first son. Brigitta married at the tender age of sixteen, and her first daughter was born exactly eight months to the day after Melissa's son was born. I envied my sisters living their cool, independent lives, having boyfriends that later became husbands, enjoying their babies and having their own homes and money to buy whatever they wanted. Of course, I imagined endless sweets, chocolate, chips and fizzy drinks. In the naivety of childhood, I had no comprehension of the struggle they faced just to pay the bills.

Instead, I dreamed of meeting my very own Prince Charming and wondered what he would look like. I imagined having a perfect family full of love, happiness and laughter. I even chose names for our babies!

My sister Ingrid was six years older than me, and I'm pretty sure she saw me as the annoying little sibling. We bickered a lot, as sisters do, and she gave me lots of 'dead arms', but she also taught me how to make pom-poms and we drew pictures together. One day she shared some wisdom with me. I'd drawn the sky as a thin blue line at the top of the page and she said, "Look out the kitchen window and you'll see the sky comes all the way down to the horizon." My childhood mind was totally blown by this revelation, and my drawings were never the same again.

I felt so privileged and grown up when Ingrid let me type on her mechanical typewriter, like a real journalist. It's funny the things you remember. Once, Ingrid typed, "Queen sux. And so does Prince." I looked up at my cool big sister, my eyes wide and sparkling with mischief. At the time I only had a vague idea who Queen and Prince were, but in our home the word 'sux' was not allowed because it was considered a naughty word, as were the words 'fart' and 'bum'. If these words were ever uttered within earshot of our parents, our punishment was a mouth washed out with soap or one smack on the bottom with an open hand, stick, rubber pipe, or a wooden spoon, followed right away by a big hug and an assurance we were loved.

I was so proud of Ingrid when she got a job working in a bank straight after leaving school. When she got off the phone, she came outside to tell Mum and I the exciting news. I looked up at my big sister and aspired to do well in school, just like she had.

* * *

One family in particular features strongly in my childhood memories. I spent a lot of time at the Palmer's home, exploring and 'hunting' in the bush behind their house and playing with a dog named Bright Eyes. It was at their house that I learned to ride a pushbike, stopping my unsteady trajectory by crashing into a garden hedge.

Edward Palmer and I were born within days of each other. There were already four boys in his family, and three girls in mine, and when we came along our mums joked about swapping us as babies. As a child I always thought we would marry someday.

I often stayed over at their place and slept on a mattress on the floor between Richard and Edward's beds. We'd talk for hours before falling asleep until one night, Mrs. Palmer came in and said I was now too old to sleep in the boys' room and had to go sleep in their younger sister, Christina's, bedroom. I didn't understand why I'd been asked to move so abruptly. I missed the company of the boys and cried myself to sleep that night.

Our adventures into the bush at the Palmer's home reminded me of Narnia in *The Lion, the Witch and the Wardrobe*. Walking into the trees to explore was thrilling. I imagined we were like the children in the book, stepping into their wardrobe and finding themselves in an entirely new world. Each journey into the bush was exciting. The boys took compasses and pocketknives, and we never knew where our imaginations would take us.

Edward recalls: "The very first memory I have of Keren was when we moved from Wairoa back to Marton. It must have been very hard on my mother, as she had recently separated from my father. In fact, the whole thing must have been hard on my entire family. I remember staying with the Maas family and meeting Keren the following morning as we had arrived very late the night before. But if I were to talk about a special time from when we were very young it would be this. Keren's father used to plant fields of maize crops as stock feed, but would plant the first few rows in corn for members of the church. I remember one evening, right on dusk, how the setting sun dimly shone dark yellow through the corn stalks and rows. Keren and I ran off together and played in the corn field while our families picked corn! You have to remember we were only five-year-olds, so young and innocent! While Keren may have been friends with my brother and sister as well, I always considered her *my* friend."

* * *

I spent a lot of time at Grandma and Grandad Maas' house in Shelton Place. I'd slide down the staircase on my bottom, pick blueberries, strawberries, blackberries and raspberries in Grandad's berry patch, and eat almost as many as I collected. I spent many happy hours playing cards and board games with Grandma. "Just one more game?" she would ask over and over. We would end up playing 'just one more game' countless times, and I loved it.

Grandad took my older sisters out white-baiting. I regret I never had the chance to experience this with him. He died when I was nine, but to this day when I catch a whiff of those little pink 'smoker' sweets, it reminds me of him.

We made many visits to Australia to see my mother's parents. They lived in the outback of Queensland, and some of my clearest memories are of the extraordinary creatures living there. Galahs and kookaburras, lorikeets and cockatoos flew freely, all so noisy with their boisterous, loud calls. Then there were the reptiles, like the frill-necked lizard who lived in a tree in the garden, and the gecko that enjoyed the cool of the fridge until I reached to open the door, saw it just before my hand touched it, and screamed, giving it such a fright that its tail fell off! Then there was the brown snake that slithered towards us as Mum and I were taking a walk one day. We yelled out to Dad, who ran to the shed, got a gun, and shot it dead just inches from our feet.

The insects in Australia were huge, and they seemed to congregate in our bedsheets. Then there were the plagues of mice and frogs. As we drove at night with the lights of Grandfather's car illuminating the darkness, the road appeared to be rippling like water as hundreds, maybe thousands, of mice covered the ground around us. Frogs would be all over the windows, porch, and paths, and once we found one boiled inside the kettle. Goodness only knows how many cups were drunk from that kettle before it was discovered. It was never a dull moment, staying at our Australian grandparents' place.

Grandma always smelled of tea tree oil, and this scent reminds me of her to this day. She crocheted around handkerchiefs, hand towels, and tea towels and gave these to us, along with doilies and crystal ornaments, for our 'hope chests' every time we saw her.

Dad's cousin Murray, his wife, Jenny, and their children lived even deeper into the Queensland outback than my grandparents, and driving there was a real adventure. Kangaroos hopped across the red, parched terrain, and I would peer out the car window searching the trees for koalas. They even had pet kangaroos, and I remember one in particular named Marty.

* * *

We had many holidays around New Zealand. I remember a boat ride travelling back to Whakatane from White Island, sitting below deck watching huge waves crash over the front of the boat while Dad vomited relentlessly into a sick bag. I was sure that if I stared through the window long enough, I would spot a shark amongst the barrage of water pummelling the boat and spraying over us.

We spent countless Saturday nights at the stock car races in Palmerston North. I remember the smell of oil mixed with dirt and tyre smoke, the ringing in our ears and vibrations in our bellies as the cars roared past the grandstand flinging dirt against the barrier fences and into the crowd, the taste of candy floss, punnets of salty chips smothered in tomato sauce, and hot dogs on a stick.

I am grateful for everything my parents did for me and for the way they raised me. They continued in the footsteps of our ancestors, building a legacy of faith. As a child, my parents protected me from the harsh realities that existed outside the sanctuary of our family home. I discovered how different life was once I left their protection. I didn't realise at the time how fortunate I was to have such great parents, a loving wider family, and such an idyllic childhood.

I thought life would always be like this. I thought everyone's family was the same. I thought all men were good, godly, family men like my dad.

In hindsight, I took so much for granted.

I shouldn't have…

2

School Years

On my first official day of school, I was so excited I tried to open the car door before we even turned the corner at the school! Nevertheless, I waited until we came to a stop on the gravel carpark, then jumped down from the brown leather seats of our 1970's Ford Falcon. As soon as my sneakers hit the stones, my five-year-old legs carried me as fast as they could through the gates and underneath the wooden sign which read: *South Makirikiri School*.

Running ahead of Mum, I headed towards Miss Sanson's junior classroom, then waited for her to hold my hand to steady me as we clambered up the steps. It was a regular occurrence for me to join the 'big school kids' while Mum and my aunty tended to the school gardens, but this day, as we approached the door of the classroom, my excitement was suddenly exchanged for shyness. I hid behind Mum's skirt as the teacher welcomed me. Miss Sanson held out her hand and led me to the painting table where large jars, filled with thick, gluggy paint, sat in the centre. I tiptoed to reach the brush in the jar of black paint. Between brush strokes, I made fleeting nervous glances across the table towards the classroom axolotl. Equal measures of curiosity, fascination, and unease coursed through my body. I wasn't sure about this strange, semi-transparent, alien-like creature who seemed to be staring right back at me from his glass aquarium.

The 'big kids' would have been only about ten years old, but I thought they were so grown up. The girls were always telling me to sit on their knee so they could give me cuddles. They fussed over me and doted on me, telling me how little and cute I was, and checking up on me. "Are you okay, Keren?" they would ask. "Do you need any help?" During one school outing, the 'big girls' argued over who would be my buddy and hold my hand as we walked to our destination.

The school was just down the road from our farm. As I got older, I rode my pushbike while my dad followed behind, painstakingly slowly, on his motorbike. It was a sight that my cousins, who also attended the school, found hilarious. My uncle and cousins pointed and laughed as they drove past.

Four generations of Maas children went to this small country school: Grandma, Dad, my sisters and I, and for a time, my two eldest daughters. In 1985, when I started attending, there were only two classrooms and about thirty students in the entire school. Miss Sanson was my teacher throughout my junior years, and the school principal, Mr. Wheeler, in my senior years. Mr. Wheeler's motto was permanently written across the top of the blackboard at the front of our class: 'Honesty in all things'.

I hated running cross-country at school. I was often lapped as we ran around the school fields, coming over the finish line in last place, often in tears, well after everyone else had finished and the spectators were walking away. But I loved swimming. I spent hours at the Ohakea Airbase pool, swimming length after length. The hard work paid off. I did well at school swimming carnivals, coming away with an impressive haul of certificates and gleaming trophies each year. I was often selected for interschool competitions, and dreamed of swimming across the Cook Strait one day, or winning a gold medal at the Olympics.

On Saturday mornings I played netball. Mum would take a carload of us girls to the dairy after the game and buy us all a raspberry bun to eat on the way home. I remember our team coming runner-up one year, quite an achievement for our modest little country school. Life was simple and innocent: no cell phones, no internet, just kids being kids, playing, imagining, exploring and having adventures.

Throughout primary school I dreamed of being an author, a journalist, a zoo keeper (so I could spend all day cuddling animals), or a marine biologist (so I could befriend dolphins and orcas). I loved writing stories. Before I could write properly, I dictated stories to Dad, who wrote them down for me. Family friends often asked me to read aloud any stories I'd written since their last visit. I sent poems to women's magazines, which were published in the children's section, and I was the only student selected from our school to attend a creative writing workshop with the famous New Zealand children's author, Margaret Mahy. In my last year of primary school, I wrote a play which was performed at the end of year prizegiving.

I finished primary school at the top of my class. On my last day at South Makirikiri Primary School, Mr. Wheeler turned to me and said, "I can't wait to see your name in print one day." He had no idea how much those words would come to mean to me.

* * *

Changing schools was a significant culture shock for me. Not only did I now have to travel about eleven kilometres into town to attend the local intermediate school, it was also the first time I'd heard swearing and experienced bullying. Friends I'd been close to for the previous six years at primary school no longer seemed to acknowledge each other, and my academic skills which had been praised at primary school, received no recognition. I was no longer the fastest swimmer, and felt unseen and lost.

The year before I started high school, my parents and I attended an open day at Sacred Heart College. We were shown around the hostel, and I was instantly captivated. I was such a fan of those coming-of-age American television shows and high school movies that made the teen years look so cool, and the whole idea of boarding school seemed so attractive, grown up and exciting. I couldn't wait to leave what was a wonderful home life to begin a new one.

Little did I know . . .

* * *

High school was rough. I was overweight and not very pretty, but I was intelligent, which made me the 'teacher's pet'. This combination made me an easy target for bullying. Sacred Heart College was an all-girls school. Until that point, I had been in co-ed schools. Now I found the girls to be catty and cruel. The constant teasing and name-calling, the nasty words . . . it still plays on my mind.

I was in the hostel's dining room one evening waiting for our turn to get our dinner. One of the senior girls was talking about how she could see the beauty in everyone. It was a lovely thought—until she pointed directly at me and said, "...even in her." The other girls at the table looked at me and screwed up their faces in disbelief as if to say, "How could anyone possibly see her as beautiful?" My heart sank, and I felt exposed. Everyone was looking at me, judging me, repulsed by my physical appearance. I felt like a social pariah. I wanted the ground to open up and swallow me.

The saying, "Sticks and stones may break my bones, but words will never hurt me," could not have been further from the truth. I now know that words can haunt us for years after they have been spoken, and without a significant healing journey, the effects of being bullied can last a lifetime. I was told with relentless consistency that I was fat and ugly, and I began to believe the negative words that were fed to me. This created a core belief that took root, germinated, and infected the very fibre of my being.

I boarded for two terms and hated it. The bullying was intense and constant, and I missed all the comforts of home, especially Mum's cooking. I lasted for half a year before moving home and becoming a day student, travelling to and from Whanganui each day on the bus— yet another place where I was constantly picked on.

During a physical education class, I was sitting behind a group of girls I envied, thinking they were cool and beautiful. They were talking about my friend, saying how ugly she was, and laughing. "Shhh, her friend's behind us," one of the girls said. This just made the others laugh even louder and one said, "I don't care. She's even uglier." In that moment, my self-esteem hit rock bottom. I began to hate myself and the way I looked. I despised my ghostly white skin, my crooked teeth and overbite, and my fat calves which girls referred to as my 'tree trunk legs'.

It didn't help that I had been raised in an environment of faith. Being in a Catholic school, I naively assumed that the students would share my beliefs, and so I was surprised to learn that the majority had never set foot inside a church. When my peers discovered I wholeheartedly believed in God and that I believed the Bible, their ridicule was immense. It was the first time I ever fully realised that not everyone believed in God, and that many people thought of the Bible as a mere fairy tale or myth. The teasing was made all the worse when I tried to appeal to reason, contending the case for God's existence and the validity of the Bible.

I took a lot of pride in my school work and achieved a high academic standard. We didn't use computers, so everything was written or drawn by hand. I spent hours on the presentation of my work, designing fancy titles and borders. I was a perfectionist. Mum would get so frustrated with me because I'd spend hours on my homework, make the tiniest mistake, throw the whole lot away, and start all over again. I was often up late at night making sure my work was just right.

My hard work was rewarded. I always did well at school prizegivings, coming away with awards for being top of the class in most subjects, including Religious Education, which was a surprise given my refusal to pray to Mary and the saints or do the rosary.

Despite being at an all-girls school, I was boy-crazy during my college years, and I had a real thing for brown boys. My attractions were unrequited, but that didn't stop me being a ditzy teenage girl. Everyone knew about my preferences—it was blindingly obvious. Every inch of my bedroom wall reflected my allure to 'brown people'. While other girls were crushing on Brad Pitt, Leonardo DiCaprio and Keanu Reeves, I had the likes of Will Smith, Larenz Tate and Warren G plastered all over my bedroom wall. I wore baggy jeans and hoodies, Starter jackets and basketball singlets, and Nike Air High Tops. I listened to hip-hop and R&B music, and loved to watch programmes like *The Fresh Prince of Bel Air*, and *South Central*. In fact, *Boyz 'n the Hood* is still my favourite movie!

I was often referred to as a 'wigga'—a derogatory term for a white person who wants to be an African American. I even tried using fake tan to remedy my ghostly white complexion, but this merely added fuel to the fire for the bullies when my skin turned orange. From then on, I was referred to as 'the orange Māori'.

Hayley was my best friend in high school. She remembers our friendship with great fondness, as do I. We would speak on the phone for ages until our parents pulled the phone plugs out of the wall, and we watched countless movies together until we fell asleep. We'd write lyrics to songs and rap them together. Hayley was so jealous when I got to have a spiral perm, but our friendship was unbreakable. She was at my house most weekends, or I was at hers. We always talked about how she was going to marry Mark Tautai and I would marry Tim Matagi (both from the New Zealand boy band, *Purest Form*). We decided we would have a double wedding and live next door to each other.

I had a number of real-life crushes during this time. Once, Hayley and I 'accidentally' missed our bus home and followed a boy called Hemi all the way to his house. Cell phones weren't a thing back then, and our fathers were looking for us all over Whanganui for hours. It was getting dark when they found us, and they were furious. It's only now, as a parent myself, that I understand their anger and worry.

Hayley, our friend Katrina and I remember 'wagging' Religious Education days to hide out on 'the track', a walkway amongst the dense trees between our school and Saint Augustine's (an all-boys school), talking in whispers to avoid being found.

I had a huge crush on Jonah Lomu, who was a New Zealand rugby player at the time. I even went so far as to have a number '11' shaved into my eyebrow to match his. In my final year of high school, Mum and Dad took me to a Blues vs Hurricanes rugby game in Palmerston North. I was star-struck watching Jonah play, and ecstatic when the Blues won 36–28. I wanted to get Lomu's autograph after the game but the crowds were crazy. My heart sank. I was sure I was going to miss out, but Mum followed him all the way to the change rooms to get my sought-after autograph. I hung it on my bedroom wall, along with the pen he had used.

My one and only boyfriend at college was Monty. Monty was a year older than me and attended St Augustine's. I got Hayley to ask Monty out for me, sure I'd rejected. I was accustomed to being told how fat and ugly I was. But I was shocked and excited when he unexpectedly said yes. Unfortunately, I was far too shy to even make eye contact with him let alone talk to him in person, so all our communication was via phone calls and notes.

One morning after I'd spent a night at Hayley's, he saved me a seat on the school bus. I was so excited about the prospect of finally being in close proximity to my very own boyfriend, and I had every intention of sitting with him, but as soon as I saw the bus approaching, all my courage was swept away by a tsunami-sized wave of nerves. My heart pounded so fast that I began to feel light-headed, my legs turned to jelly, and I wanted to run away and hide. As I climbed onto the bus, I hung my head, looked at the floor, and proceeded to sit right up the front of the bus without even acknowledging Monty.

For weeks after, I was kicking myself for not sitting with him when I'd promised him on the phone the night before that I would. I felt so guilty and rude. I despised my overwhelming shyness and awkwardness. Despite our complete lack of face-to-face interaction, I was constantly daydreaming about hand-holding, first kisses, falling in love, getting married, and living happily ever after. My imagination created entire scenarios which reality by no means replicated.

Hayley and I had only one falling out during high school, but it lasted almost half a year. I was ousted from our circle of friends. Girls I had been close to pointed at me, whispered, sniggered, gave nasty looks, or simply walked past me as if I was invisible. I was devastated. I had no one to turn to. I spent morning tea and lunch breaks alone in the school library, or hiding away in the toilets waiting for the bell to ring signalling a return to class, where I sat alone.

I dreaded going to school each day because I felt like an outcast. I cried to Mum and Dad, begging them to let me drop out so I could be home-schooled. I knew I could concentrate on my studies far better at home because I was intelligent, focused, and well-organised. Mum, Dad and I met with the school counsellor, and as a result, my parents insisted I stay in school, not wanting me to develop a habit of running away from my problems just as I had when I desperately wanted to attend boarding school, then left soon after.

The emotional turmoil of daily rejection and exclusion soon took its toll, until one day I walked right out the school gate and kept going. I didn't know where I was going, but I knew I had to get away from it all. I found myself on the Dublin Street bridge in Whanganui. Three girls in uniforms from another high school were walking towards me on the bridge. When they came close, one of the girls punched me in the nose. She was wearing knuckle-busters, and blood went everywhere. She pushed me up against the railing. I thought she was going to push me over into the river until one of the other girls told her to leave me alone.

I was in shock. I'd never experienced violence before. I didn't know these girls. It was a random attack and I didn't know what to do. I cupped my hands under my chin to catch the blood which by now was pouring from my nose, drenching my school jacket. People driving across the bridge looked at me, but no one stopped to offer help.

I crossed the bridge and went into the restrooms at Kowhai Park, shaking and crying, and tried to clean myself up. I thought about going to one of the homes across from the park to ask for help, but at that moment my faith in other humans was so low, and I was afraid that knocking on the wrong door could bring even more trouble. I waited for my nose to stop bleeding, then shakily made my way to a bus stop to catch the bus home. Hayley was at the bus stop when I got there. We hadn't spoken in weeks, but when she saw me, our falling out was momentarily forgotten, and she rushed over to see if I was all right. When I got home, Mum was shocked by all the blood on my jacket and uniform but I refused to tell her what happened.

It took a long time for Hayley and I to repair our friendship. We were walking along the sidewalk one day some time later. As we were talking and laughing, a hefty-looking woman strode up to me and demanded to know what I was looking at. I hadn't even noticed her until she spoke to me. "That's what I want to know," I replied without thinking. With that, she punched me in the jaw. The taste of blood filled my mouth and I immediately regretted making the smart-assed reply that was so typical of the everyday banter I enjoyed with my older sister.

It began to feel like trouble was out to find me wherever I went.

3

Shattered Innocence

"Hayley! Hayley!" I whispered. "Check out those cute guys!" We peeped out a bedroom window at my sister Brigitta's house and were immediately captivated by the boys in the backyard next door. One of them had his head shaved on the sides and back. His remaining long hair on top was parted in the middle and plaited into two thick braids, making Hayley and I think of a guy from one of our favourite hip-hop groups. If looks were anything to go by, these were exactly our type. We just had to know who they were. Too shy to approach them ourselves, we wrote a letter and asked my little niece to deliver it over the fence, while we continued to cower under the window, peering over the sill to see them read it. To this day, I cannot recall what we wrote and shudder to think of the ditzy teenage drivel that note must have contained. We probably even folded it into one of those origami love hearts that we thought were so cool back in the '90s.

My memory fails me as to how we arranged to meet up, but a day or two later, Hayley and I made our way to Brigitta's house once again, this time when no-one was home. Hayley gave me a leg-up so I could clamber through a high window into the lounge and unlock the house. The boys came over, and all I can remember is not knowing what to say to them. I was beyond awkward and couldn't stop giggling when John and his cousin, Wiki, were in the house. I overheard Wiki saying that he called dibs on "the one in the checked pants." He didn't even know my friend's name, but I still couldn't help but feel that John got lumped with the consolation prize.

Despite our start, John and I quickly became a couple. I felt like I'd hit the jackpot. John was eighteen, and I had just turned sixteen. After years of being told I was fat and ugly, and having guys show absolutely no interest in me, I had a boyfriend who personified the image I romanticised—that of a cute Māori boy.

John and I spent as much time together as possible over the following months, either at our farm or at his parents' house. He would often arrive in a taxi to pick me up and take me into town to his mum and dad's place, but we would always return to our own houses at night.

When we weren't together, we talked on the phone for hours. When we ran out of things to say, we stayed on the line together in silence. As a farming contractor, Dad needed to keep the phone free for work, and our lengthy calls angered my parents so much they would pull the phone cord from the wall.

I remember our first kiss, my first ever, under the carport, against the wooden railing, in front of his parents' yellow Falcon. We were waiting for Dad to pick me up when John leaned towards me. I knew he was going to kiss me, and I felt shy and anxious and turned away. He lifted my chin with such tenderness and kissed me gently. It was perfect. I felt as though I was floating on air.

I loved cuddling on his bed, our legs entwined, bodies close and fitting together as if we were made for each other. I kept pinching myself, unable to believe I had a boyfriend, especially one as good looking as John. He was kind, caring, thoughtful.

I lost my virginity to John on my sister's couch. Brigitta had given me a 'girl talk' the afternoon before it happened, handing me condoms and even showing me how to use them. She told me that her door would be shut all night and assured me that the walls were soundproof. I appreciated her talking to me so openly, but I was so embarrassed, and I couldn't stop giggling. I had been taught that sex before marriage was a sin, but I was so desperate to be wanted and loved that I gave in. Even mid-deed I remember thinking, *This is wrong. I shouldn't be doing this,* but I justified it with the thought that John and I would marry one day soon, and then I would ask God to forgive me for not having waited.

Excelling at school had always been a priority for me, but John was now my sole focus, and everything changed. I became rude and obnoxious to teachers and neglected my school work. I was even put 'on report', something I never could have imagined happening. This shocked my classmates, who had always known me to be top of the class and the teacher's pet. I blew my chances of achieving top marks in my School Certificate—in fact, I barely passed most subjects. I failed Accounting miserably because I simply got up and walked out of the exam after half an hour to spend time with John and Wiki across the road at Virginia Lake.

I went back to school the following year, but only stayed a few days before dropping out. Leaving home, I moved in with John at his parents' home. It was just months after we first met, but we had fun together. I have a memory of him running across the train tracks with me on his shoulders, and lying together on the benches at Wilson Park, looking up at the stars and satellites passing by. The experience of first love was special and magical. I was so in love. I had found the man I wanted to spend the rest of my life with. My fairy tale had come true.

I was shocked to find that John regularly broke into his parents' bedroom through a hole in the ceiling above his wardrobe to steal money. I found it even stranger that John wouldn't let me go next door to visit my sister Brigitta. "Your sister won't want you bothering her," he said. He told me this so often that I believed he was right. Soon I began feeling guilty about wanting to spend time with my family rather than with him.

John and I had been living together for several weeks when I found he had lied to me about his name and age. His real name was Dion and he wasn't eighteen at all. He was twenty-one. Did it matter? I was surprised, and wondered why he had lied. *Who is this old man I am living and sleeping with?* I wondered. *Do I even know him at all?*

It didn't matter. I loved him.

* * *

Soon Dion and I moved in to our own flat. We slept on old foam squabs that his parents gave us. They were two high and two wide and came apart during the night so we'd end up on the cold wooden floor between them. Mum and Dad let me take my chest of drawers for our clothes, and we had a table in the lounge, along with a second-hand washing machine and a fridge. That was it.

We gave each other tattoos with green Indian ink and sewing pins. He tattooed his name in a banner with a heart and a cross on my wrist, and a 'D' for Dion below my left eye. He tattooed my name on his hand, and I gave him a letter 'K' for Keren below his left eye.

Whenever he went out, I would wait for him to get home, watching by the window to see him walking up the road. He thought it was so sweet. He became so emotional one time when he spotted me in the window. A smile spread over his face, he broke into a run, flew through the front door, fell onto his knees before me, hugged me, and burst into tears.

"You're so cute!" he said. "I love you so much!" I started crying tears of joy too. I knelt down with him and we hugged on the floor for ages. Despite his profession of undying love for me, however, he didn't like being seen with me in public. He would disguise himself by putting his hoodie on and wearing sunglasses. Even then, he made me walk on the opposite side of the road because he was so ashamed to be seen with me. Once, we drove out of town with his parents to go to the garage sales. He made me lie down in the back seat the entire time so no one could see me, and I wasn't allowed out of the car once we got there. His parents turned a blind eye. This hurt a lot, but when we were at home alone, he was so loving and affectionate that I somehow seemed to forget how ugly and worthless he had made me feel.

I didn't know much about Dion when we first met. I knew he drank because he and Wiki brought bottles of beer to Brigitta's house when we first met. They offered Hayley and I some but we declined. I had never tasted alcohol before (except for a few cheeky mouthfuls at my sister's wedding when I was about thirteen), but now that we had moved into our own home, we began to drink regularly. I remember the first time I tried drinking whiskey. Dion was out, and I didn't know you were supposed to mix it with something else. I drank over half a bottle straight, and was a total mess by the time he got home.

Then there was the strange smell in the house, one I hadn't known before. It was often there when I came out of the bathroom after a shower. I liked it. It was sweet and piney and I thought it was coming from a tree in the backyard. It took me a while to find out what the smell was.

We often spent the day in the bedroom because we had no furniture in the lounge. Dion confined me to our room when his friends or family visited. When he heard them at the door, he jumped out of bed, gave me a kiss and said he'd be back soon, before leaving and shutting the door behind him.

One afternoon, I decided to come out. I walked into the kitchen and found Dion and his cousin doing something on the stove. Dion was flustered when he saw me, and he panicked. Cutlery clanged and objects fell to the floor as he tried to hide everything. His cousin said something like, "Doesn't she know?"

After she left, he came into the bedroom, got down on his knees beside the bed, apologised, and begged for forgiveness. I asked questions and he explained that I had walked in on him smoking cannabis, using knives heated on the element to create fumes.

I was totally thrown. My sheltered childhood had not prepared me for this. I didn't even know people in New Zealand used drugs, thinking that such things only existed in 'big bad America', and now the voice in my head spoke with even greater clarity: *Why is he lying to me? Who is this man that I am living with and whose name I have tattooed on my body for life? Do I even know him at all?* This time, I paid a little more attention to that inner voice. I began to wonder if Dion was indeed the type of man I envisaged spending my life with.

It took me a while to accept that Dion was using drugs but when push came to shove, it didn't matter. I loved him, and it wasn't long before I asked if I could try it because I was curious. Dion was hesitant and asked me several times if I was sure. I was. Suddenly, I acquired an entirely new vocabulary, using words like tinny, cap, oil, goldie, spot, joint, sesh and bong, as if I'd always talked that way.

After smoking we often had 'the munchies', and our favourite concoction was strawberry ice-cream all whipped up, covered in cereal, with Coca-Cola poured over the top.

I soon learned that Dion owed money to his dealer, and one day she came to the house demanding that he pay up. Dion made all sorts of excuses and promises, then she said, "Do you want me to go in there and beat up that little girlfriend of yours?" As soon as I heard that, I jumped out of bed, ran to the bathroom and locked myself inside. When Dion saw I'd been hiding, he laughed. "You know I'd never let anyone hurt you, babe," he assured me.

* * *

After seven months, we moved back to Dion's parents' home. Our debts were growing, and I wanted to save money for furniture, but we continued drinking and smoking. We 'spotted' on the kitchen stove or the gas heater in the lounge when his parents went out. I remember one session with Dion and his sister. I was sitting on the kitchen bench. I knew I'd had enough, but he kept saying, "Just one more, babe." As I inhaled the smoke, yet again, through the funnel he handed me, I fell forward off the bench. Dion caught me mid-air and carried me to bed. I was only semi-conscious, but I knew what was going on around me.

One night I became violently ill after drinking just half a can of beer. A pregnancy test the following day revealed I was pregnant. We were both so happy. Dion was sweet and caring, waiting on me hand and foot. He wouldn't let me lift a finger. We talked about baby names, imagining our precious child, and how he or she would look. He liked the name Ngahuiamaia for a girl and Shaka Zulu for a boy. I liked Tatyana and Zion.

I gave up drinking and smoking dope when I learned I was pregnant. For several weeks Dion was attentive and loving, but then things began to change. I can't pinpoint the exact moment when everything went wrong. All I know is that my world began to shatter, like glass breaking in slow motion.

There were nights when he would not let me sleep. He shook and shoved me all night long to keep me awake, mocking and imitating me when I cried.

As the baby grew and pressure on my bladder increased, I had to go to the toilet more often. Sometimes Dion wouldn't let me go for hours, pushing me back down when I tried to get up. Pinning me to the bed, he would push on my bladder and taunt me, saying, "Aw, do you need to go to the toilet? Are you going to wet yourself?" Then he would kneel on my pregnant tummy, bouncing up and down over and over so his knees hit my stomach, sharp, hard and deep. "I hope the baby dies," he said. Afterwards, he would panic and cry, hug and kiss my belly, and ask if I still felt the baby moving inside.

Dion started teasing me about my looks, my teeth in particular, imitating my overbite, and calling me 'goofy'. We fought often—and loud. If our fight was too full-on and Dion's mother was home from work, she would call my parents and they would come and pick me up. One time, Dion wrestled the phone away from her to stop her calling my parents, hitting her over the head with the receiver.

Dion's brother only got involved once. We were in the lounge, a rare occasion for us. I was on the couch, and Dion was punching me. His brother rushed in and pulled Dion off, giving me a chance to get out from underneath him. I ran out the back door, crossed the road, and knocked on the door of a random house. The lady let me in to call Dad, who picked me up.

I lived between Dion's home in town, and on the farm with Mum and Dad. At his house, Dion and I rarely left our bedroom. He had given me strict instructions not to talk to his parents or siblings, nor was I allowed to make eye contact with them. I had to walk in the door and go straight to the bedroom. When I got home after spending a day or two at Mum and Dad's I always felt extremely rude walking past his family without giving them any acknowledgment, but Dion said they didn't want me to talk to them. I was not allowed to eat with them or sit in the lounge to watch TV. If I wore a dress, Dion accused me of trying to impress his brothers.

Aunties, uncles and cousins came by, and there were drunken parties that often ended in fights. Because I was not allowed out of the bedroom, I never saw them, but I heard them. Sometimes, Dion's six-year-old niece was there while the parties were going on. When the fights started, she would run into our room crying. One night, I heard Dion's mum and dad screaming at each other. Dion's niece was in bed with us. Both she and I were terrified by the commotion. Dion had his arms around us both, hugging and comforting us, trying to cover our ears. I was shaken to see blood all over the bathroom the following morning.

Mum rang one day, wanting to take me to Palmerston North for a day of shopping with my sister, Melissa. Dion always listened to my phone calls, his ear pressed hard against the back of the receiver. He whispered to me, "Can I come too?" When I asked Mum, she said, no it was a girls' day out. Dion kept motioning for me to ask if he could go with us, but Mum was adamant in her refusal. I felt caught in the middle and knew what would happen when I hung up the phone. I was terrified.

In my trepidation, helplessness, and panic, two words then came from my mouth, words I never imagined I would say to the mother who raised me, loved me, and gave me such a wonderful childhood. "F— you!" I said, and slammed the phone down.

My behaviour horrified and sickened me. How could I be so disrespectful to my mum? I feel the guilt to this day. The sadness, shame, and confusion I felt was soon beaten out of me, however, as Dion began pummelling me with his fists, accusing me of telling Mum not to let him come shopping with us, and insisting that I was wanting to 'get up to something' in Palmerston North. I wanted so much to spend time with Mum and Melissa. It had been so long since I'd had a girly day. Instead, I did not go. I was trapped in the bedroom with a man who was violent and full of rage.

We rarely ventured from the bedroom at Dion's parents' house, but one day when his parents were out, Dion decided we would lie in the backyard and sunbathe. Time outdoors was rare, and I enjoyed feeling the sunshine on my skin and breathing in the fresh air. We talked and laughed, cuddled and kissed, as we soaked up the afternoon sunshine.

When Dion's parents arrived home, they looked at us with surprise because we were out of the bedroom. They gave an instinctive "Hello!" and I responded with a smile and a "Hi!" In a flash, Dion's demeanour changed. His eyes were fierce. "Don't talk to them," he said. "They don't want you to talk to them. Who do you think you are? Stop being so nosey." We stayed outdoors until my face began to sting, adding to the misery of the worthlessness and sadness that plagued me. I asked Dion if we could go back inside and he said no. We remained in the sun.

That evening my entire face came out in blisters. This was no ordinary sunburn. I looked like something out of a horror movie. Even Mum recoiled when she saw me the following day. The blisters were large and full of fluid. My face burned and I was in terrible pain. Mum took me to the doctor, who was shocked that the sun alone could cause such burns.

* * *

In spite of the abuse, I loved knowing a precious, tiny human was growing inside me. I loved to feel the baby kicking. Sometimes we could even make out the shape of a little hand or a foot outlined on my tummy. We'd place objects on top of my tummy and marvel at how baby would kick them right off. I loved going to appointments with my midwife and hearing our little one's heartbeat or seeing our baby on the ultrasound screen. Pregnancy is a beautiful miracle. I loved the sacredness of carrying inside me a part of the man I loved.

For nine months, however, I was plagued by morning sickness. I lost weight and was under a specialist who gave me medication to help with nausea. But one night, I had a serious and terrifying reaction to the medication and lost control of my body. I felt like I was possessed. My mouth opened so wide my jaw hurt, and I couldn't close it. My legs and arms kept tightening and contorting. Dion phoned a doctor who came to the house and gave me an injection that stopped it.

We moved into our own place again to await the birth of our first baby, but the abuse intensified. Dion began stealing my EFTPOS card, then sneaking out in the middle of the night while I was sleeping to withdraw my 'benefit' money. I hid my card but he hit and threatened me until I gave it to him. *Maybe things will be different once our baby is born,* I thought. *Maybe the moment he lays eyes on our precious newborn, his heart will be transformed through love for her. Maybe once we become a family, Dion will change...*

4

Broken Dreams

From childhood I dreamed of becoming a mum, of having a family filled with love and happiness. Now, as I marvelled at my growing belly, it was surreal to think that there was a real live baby in there. I couldn't wait to meet her, to see what she looked like, to cuddle, kiss and adore her.

Our beautiful first daughter was born on a Tuesday afternoon in July. I was seventeen, and Dion was twenty-three. We named our baby girl Janaya.

Janaya made a swift arrival. Dion witnessed her birth, along with my mum. When I held my baby in my arms, I was overwhelmed by a love so powerful as to be almost without description. I looked at her little face, tiny fingers and toes. She was perfect. I had never before felt a love like what I had for my precious baby girl. I couldn't believe someone so beautifully immaculate had come from me, and I was in awe of her. I wanted to stare at her forever. In that moment, I loved being a mum.

When we brought Janaya home from the hospital, Dion helped with nappy changing and propped up my arm with his when I was breastfeeding.

One day he made a flippant comment about pinning our baby against a wall and using a gun on her. It shook me to the core, but I felt powerless to confront him. Then one evening, when Janaya was about six weeks old, we were giving her a bath when Dion said, "Look at her leg."

I noticed that Janaya's left leg was floating limply in the water. When I lifted her out of the water, her leg just hung there while she kicked her right leg around as usual. Dion then told me that when I was in bed, Janaya was on the loungeroom floor kicking, and flinging her arms around, when he heard a click. I gently moved her leg and could feel it clicking. Janaya was content and not in obvious pain, but I was concerned, and wanted to take her to the doctor right away. Dion would not let me.

Janaya seemed her normal self, but when my sister, Melissa, visited over the weekend and I pointed out Janaya's leg, she freaked out and asked me how it happened. I told her I didn't know. Melissa came back the following morning and told me I'd better take Janaya to the doctor. Somehow she managed to get us to the doctor without Dion stopping us. When an x-ray revealed that her leg was broken, I burst into tears and my legs almost gave way beneath me. I was heartbroken. How could I have not known? She was so tiny; she must have been in so much pain. What sort of mother was I not to notice sooner?

Janaya was in hospital for the next month, her legs in traction and her tiny body dangled over a cot. I breastfed her standing upright and leaning over the top of her. I stayed with our baby until Dion got angry. He didn't like that I was allowed to stay with her and he wasn't, and insisted I stay with him at the Mauri Ora accommodation. I hated being away from Janaya, and the thought of her being all alone in the hospital broke my heart, but I went along with it.

Dion and I were taken to the police station and questioned about Janaya's broken leg. The whole experience was scary and overwhelming. It was just like you see in the movies—we were separated and taken into different rooms that were bare and drab. I sat across the table from the detective while a video camera recorded our conversation. The investigator was persistent and asked a lot of questions. I told him I did not know how Janaya's leg got broken, that I knew nothing until Dion pointed it out when we were bathing her. I got the impression he thought I was lying.

We were seen by countless social workers while we were in the hospital, all trying to ascertain how Janaya's injury came about. They ran through a number of scenarios, asking if maybe her leg had been caught in bedding, or perhaps she'd fallen off a bed and someone had instinctively grabbed her leg to catch her. We told them that we honestly had no idea how it happened.

When we realised that the child protection services were considering removing our precious baby from our care, I was devastated. We were so frightened of losing Janaya, and everyone was pointing the finger at us. Dion concocted a plan, telling me to say that Janaya's leg had got caught in her bassinette as I, half asleep, pulled her into bed with me to feed her. When asked why I had not divulged this information before, I said I was scared Dion would be angry at me if he knew I'd hurt our baby.

We thought that if we could come up with a story of how Janaya's leg was broken unintentionally, they would leave us alone. This ploy was not effective, however. We lost custody of Janaya. When our baby was discharged from hospital, she was to live at Mum and Dad's. I went to live there too.

Many years later, I found some notations in our court records that took me back to the anguish I'd felt while in the hospital:

"The injury sustained requires large force of a rotational nature ..."

"Dion ... will not allow Keren to speak. He does all the talking. Dion limits family access to Janaya while in hospital."

"The paternal grandparents ... believe Dion and Keren need counselling and that Dion is very possessive of Keren."

The medical statements also made me wonder how I ever put up with such treatment:

"I have been concerned about Dion's apparent controlling attitude of Keren, and all staff have commented about how Dion will whisper in Keren's ear and tell her how to answer questions and is very reluctant to let Keren out of his sight. He also constantly closes the curtains to baby's room so the staff are not able to see what is going on. He has been told he must leave the curtain open unless Keren is breastfeeding baby."

"Keren told nursing staff ... that Dion had hit her that morning."

"Dion appears to actively discourage any visiting from Keren's family or his parents."

And then there was this statement:

"Janaya Maas ... is a child who is suffering, or is likely to suffer, ill-treatment, neglect, deprivation, abuse or harm."

* * *

At my parents' house, I spent hours and hours talking to Janaya, singing and dancing with her, reading, doing puzzles, building blocks, teaching her colours, animal noises and more. She flourished with all this time and attention and started talking early. I loved her little baby language.

Dion was allowed to come out to the farm to visit us, but again, he was angry because I spent every day and night with Janaya and he could not. I felt guilty even though it was not my fault. He often made me stay in town with him, and on those nights, I left Janaya with Mum and Dad. I hated leaving her, but I was scared of what Dion would do if I defied him.

Part of the court order was that Mum and Dad were required to drop Janaya off at Dion's parents' house on a regular basis, so they could spend time with her. I was very apprehensive about this. I was proud of the way I was brought up and wanted Janaya to have the same sort of happy childhood memories I had—or as much as possible, given all the upheaval and drama. I did not want Janaya raised around the partying and violence, but it was hard to avoid. I once approached Dion's parents about the language they used in front of Janaya, and their reply was, "We're not going to change for no one!"

* * *

Janaya and I moved from my parents' farm to my sister, Melissa's, house in town, where we stayed in her sleepout. I had access to a walk-in wardrobe, where I kept an abundant stock of baby food and nappies. Dion was allowed to see Janaya at the town library across from his house on the condition that we were not to leave the library and could not take Janaya to his house. Dion kept to these rules without any aggression.

One afternoon, after meeting Dion at the library, I got back 'home' and realised my EFTPOS card was missing. I knew right away Dion had taken it and that I had to get it back before he took the money I needed to buy food and nappies.

I was not allowed to take Janaya to Dion's house, so I rushed into my sister's kitchen where I found Melissa cooking dinner. I asked her where my nephew Riki was, hoping he might play with Janaya for five minutes while I went to get my card back before Dion withdrew money. Melissa yelled at me. "You're not using my son just so you can go and have sex with your boyfriend!" With no time to waste, I picked up Janaya and went to Dion's house. I knocked on the door, then, determined not to break any rules, went back to the footpath and called to Dion to come out. He came out and gave me my card, but when I went back to Melissa's house, she met me in the driveway and told me she had called the child protection services.

I was feeding Janaya in the sleep-out when the social workers arrived. Janaya and I were chatting away and she was smiling and giggling. The social worker took her straight out of her highchair and said they were taking Janaya back to Mum and Dad's. Janaya screamed and reached out to me crying, "Mum! Mum!" I was crying too. I felt sick. When I asked if I could go to Mum and Dad's with her, they said no. Feeling helpless, I watched the car pull out of the driveway. I could still hear Janaya crying as they drove away. It felt like my entire world had fallen apart. With tears streaming down my face, I walked around to Dion's house. When he opened the door, I told him Janaya had been taken away, then fell into his arms crying. He wrapped his arms around me and held me tight.

* * *

From that point on, I lived with him again. Janaya went to live with my sister, Ingrid, and her husband in Palmerston North. Dion and I were allowed supervised time with Janaya at a Barnados Centre there, but it was awkward having a lady following us around as we played with our daughter.

One of the agreements we had in place was that there would be a period of time between Janaya's pick up and drop off times so our paths did not cross with Ingrid and her husband. After one of our supervised visits with Janaya, Dion thought my sister and her husband had parked somewhere they shouldn't have. He was so upset, and became aggressive on our drive back to Marton to the point where I took off my seatbelt, opened the door of the car, and jumped out onto the side of the road. Dion was furious. He stopped a few metres down the road and dragged me back into the car. I was screaming and desperately trying to get my footing. It felt like my scalp was being ripped off as he aggressively pulled me along the gravel by my hair. I remember seeing people drive past, but no one stopped to help. I was trapped with him.

Dion and I were together for four-and-a-half years. I remember the traumatic events I endured but cannot be certain of when they took place as my memories are muddled by the trauma. Some memories are too horrific to recount.

He often tried to suffocate me, putting a pillow over my face and laying on top of it with all his weight bearing down on me. I struggled frantically, trying to get out from under him to gasp air. My lungs felt like they were going to explode, and many times I thought I was going to die.

Dion once tied me up to the bed using an extension cord. He gagged me using a tea towel. He shoved the tea towel so hard into my mouth that the corners of my lips ripped and bled. The tea towel was so far down my throat that I was choking and struggling to breathe. Dion paced up and down at the foot of the bed, ranting and raving like a maniac about wishing there were police and helicopters and TV cameras outside our bedroom window so they could see him cut me into pieces.

I woke up every morning with a sense of dread, never knowing if or when I would be punched, kicked, thrown around, dragged by my hair, suffocated, strangled, gagged, or have my arms and legs bent, twisted and almost broken.

I wasn't allowed to go to the toilet without his permission. He often made me wait hours before I could go. I was not allowed to shower or eat when I wanted, and often went entire days without food. I could not leave the house, or even check the mailbox or hang washing on the line.

Dion became agitated when anyone from my family visited. I closed the lounge doors whenever they came so he could listen at the door to make sure I wasn't saying anything I shouldn't. Even with him listening, he still hounded me with questions and accusations after they left. It was the same whenever I wanted to visit my family or attend family gatherings. I had to fight to get out the door, and I always feared the consequences when I returned.

Dion usually managed to inflict injuries on places of my body which could easily be concealed by my clothing or hair. It was common for my arms and legs to be black and blue under my baggy clothing, but occasionally, in his rage, he'd forget and hit me in the face. I constantly had to lie to people about the cause of my bruises, knowing that if anyone found out, I was likely to receive more. I remember having a black eye and telling my parents that I walked into a tree branch while walking through a wooded area beside the local stream.

When he went out, Dion would lock me in the bathroom. Other times, when we left the house, I had to walk with my head down. Dion often told me how ugly I was, and that people looked at me strangely when I went out in public because I was so hideous. I believed him and imagined I could see people cringe, repulsed by the sight of me in the street. If I did happen to look up for just a second, he would accuse me of looking at other guys and I would be beaten when we got home.

* * *

When I was little, I dreamed of my Prince Charming, but my childhood dreams looked nothing like the reality I was living. This was not how I envisaged true love. My dad never spoke to or treated my mum in this way. I wondered if this was to be my lot in life. Would this be it from now on? I wished my skin was brown, not ghostly white. I wanted my teeth to be perfect, not crooked and bucked. I wanted to be thinner, or beautiful, thinking maybe then he wouldn't hurt me.

I thought about leaving, but Dion had made it clear that if I ever left him, he would kill my entire family. He said he'd hunt me down and kill me too. "I may not do it straight away," he said. "It may be years later when you think I've forgotten all about it, but one day, I will turn up out of the blue to fulfil my promise."

He told me a friend was watching the house while he was at work. He said his friend had a gun and would shoot me if I tried to leave the house. I believed him. From then on, I was too scared to go anywhere near the front door and I spent my days in the bedroom where I read books and did cross-stitch. I remember lying on our bed looking out the bedroom window, watching birds flying by and envying their freedom to come and go as they pleased.

Walking home after grocery shopping one day, we got into an argument. I could tell Dion had flipped a switch. Knowing that I would be severely beaten as soon as we got indoors, I stopped walking and refused to walk any further. I didn't know what else to do. In response, Dion grabbed my hair in his fist and pulled me. I fell forward onto the ground and screamed as he dragged me along the footpath. I was terrified. If he was this violent in public, what would he be capable of if he got me home behind closed doors? I remember him dragging me right past the Marton police station, yet no one came to my aid. *Did anyone care?* I wondered. *Did my life mean that little?*

Back home, I tried to escape, to get to the door when he was beating me, but he pushed me down and kicked me. It was futile, so eventually I gave up, letting my body go limp as his rage continued. I prayed, asking God to give him a heart attack so he would die and the abuse would stop. There were times I thought about killing him in his sleep. Either that, or killing myself so I could escape him.

I prayed and hoped Mum and Dad would turn up in the middle of a fight so I could escape with them, and often they did, but as soon as Dion heard the knock on the door he would pin me down and cover my mouth so I couldn't scream until he heard the car drive away. Then when he was sure they'd gone, he'd continue to beat me.

After each fight he made me follow him around the house because he was worried I would leave. If he went to the toilet, I had to go with him and sit on the floor beside him.

We often had sex after a fight. Dion would cry, hold me tight and stroke my hair, tell me how much he loved me, say he was so sorry and that it would never happen again, then promise to change. I believed him because I so desperately wanted it to be true.

There were good times between his moments of violence, but they became few and far between. Things were usually pretty chilled out when we drank together. We listened to good music and we did have some happy times together, taking trips to the river, visiting the farm, swimming, or hanging out at the local playground. He even asked me to teach him how to cross-stitch, and we spent hours stitching together. It was endearing to see this angry, aggressive guy chilling out and concentrating on counting stitches, delicately pulling the needle and thread through the aida cloth to create intricate pictures.

One night I drank too much and vomited in my sleep. I awoke to Dion carefully lifting my head off the soiled pillow to remove it from beneath me, then gently wiping my face with a damp cloth. After cleaning the pillowcase, he climbed into bed, kissed my forehead, and asked if I was okay. If only our entire relationship was that loving and compassionate.

There were two versions of Dion, and at any moment he could switch from one to the other.

* * *

When I was nineteen, I fell pregnant with our second child. Again, Dion was gentle for a few weeks, waiting on me hand and foot, not even letting me carry grocery bags. It didn't last long though and the violence continued.

This was at the turn of the century. The world was grappling with the threat of what was called Y2K—a potential issue where the year 2000 may not be recognised by computer systems. There was much speculation about what might happen if computers around the world read the numerals 00 as the year 1900, rather than 2000. No one knew if power would be cut, banks would lose all their records, cars with date-dependent chips would work, or planes might fall out of the sky! My dad stocked up on non-perishable food and supplies, and withdrew all his money from the bank, burying thousands of dollars in the garden 'just in case'. The uncertainty over the extent to which the year 2000 would affect the world was exciting to me.

On New Year's Eve, Dion and I were parked on top of a hill overlooking the city to see in the New Year. I wondered if we'd witness Whanganui being plunged into darkness as the clock ticked over to midnight. A strange mix of trepidation and excitement had me buzzing. Unfortunately, before the climax of midnight came, something set Dion off and he began beating me right there in the car. He was particularly volatile that night, unrelenting. It was not the way I'd imagined seeing the new millennium in. Eventually the beating petered out and I realised that midnight had been and gone and the electricity hadn't cut out, I couldn't see any planes falling from the sky, and our car still worked and got us back home to Marton.

Obviously, the year 2000 came and went without a hitch. One day soon after, I was at Mum and Dad's place cuddling Janaya on the couch when my sister, Ingrid, arrived to pick her up. As soon as she walked in the door, Janaya sat up, reached out her arms to my sister and said, "Mum!" Ingrid lifted Janaya up, and I went to the bedroom and cried. Ingrid came in soon after but nothing she said could comfort me. I was inconsolable. My daughter had been taken from me because of her abusive father, and now she thought her aunty was her mum.

My life was a mess. Dreams of having the perfect, happy, loving family had been shattered. It wasn't Ingrid's fault, and I will be forever grateful to my family for stepping up and taking Janaya in. If they hadn't, I have no doubt our daughter would have ended up in foster care.

* * *

Our precious second daughter was born later that year in the early hours on a Wednesday morning in June. I was nineteen and Dion was twenty-five. We named her Sanjanah.

Dion was present. I wanted my mum to be there as she had been at Janaya's birth, but Dion said no.

When the midwife placed our second daughter in my arms, time stood still. I saw her little face for the first time, marvelled at her teeny tiny fingers and toes, and was again overwhelmed by feelings of immense love and awe. She was innocence and goodness personified. My heart was so full. Dion and I made gorgeous babies together.

I just wanted to stare and study every feature of my baby—her perfectly smooth skin, her hair as soft as silk, her brown eyes so bright and knowing. I passed her over to Dion while I had a shower, then gave her a breastfeed before leaving as the health centre did not have facilities for overnight stays.

I needed to go home and rest, but Dion insisted we take Sanjanah to meet his family. It was the middle of the night, and I sat in their dining room, sore and exhausted, as they cuddled her. The next morning, Mum and Dad brought Janaya to meet her baby sister. Janaya stared at her intently and would not let anyone else hold her. She adored her sister.

Despite their concerns about Janaya's safety around Dion, the social workers allowed Sanjanah to remain in our care. By now, Janaya had moved back to Mum and Dad's place, and Dion and I were allowed visits with her alone in our home. Things weren't going well, however. I have a vivid memory of my sweet little two-year-old, Janaya, wrapping her chubby little arms around me and using her body to shield my head while I cowered on the floor as Dion hit me repetitively. Such a brave and protective baby. She should never have seen that.

I remember one day Janaya wouldn't eat all her lunch and Dion got right in her face, nose to nose, and yelled at her to eat. Janaya was petrified, and I was terrified of what he might do to her. I grabbed her away from him and held her close. Dion said I was babying her and that she would never learn.

Sanjanah was a delightful baby but it was difficult to settle her during the night. She fell asleep while feeding but woke as soon as I took her off the breast. I was exhausted, so I appreciated when Dion would take her into the lounge and walk around with her until she fell asleep. I asked Dion how he got her to sleep so quickly, but he wouldn't tell me, and told me to figure it out for myself.

Once, I noticed something strange. When Dion brought Sanjanah back into our bedroom to tuck her into the bassinet beside me, she was making short gasping noises. When I sat up to look at her, her lips were bluish-grey. I picked her up, but her body was limp and floppy, and she was unable to hold her head up, and when I talked to her, she didn't react in her usual way. I panicked, but Dion said, "She's fine," and rolled over and went to sleep. I didn't know what was wrong with her or what to do.

I found Sanjanah in this condition again in her bassinette one day. I got her up and tried to feed her, but she wouldn't drink. It was as if she was trying to cry, but no sound came out when she opened her mouth. She was gasping for breath. I walked up and down, trying to comfort and settle her. When I showed Dion he said, "She'll snap out of it soon." Thankfully, Mum and Dad happened to turn up that day after church and I took Sanjanah out to the car. When they saw how limp and lifeless her body was, they said they would take us to the doctor. I went inside to get her car seat and tell Dion where we were going, but he said that we would walk to the doctor's surgery ourselves. I should have gone with my parents because after they left, Dion refused to let us go.

It was one night when Sanjanah was about four months old, that I walked into the lounge and caught Dion blowing in her face. As soon as he saw me, he stopped. I took her from him and took her back to bed with me. I realised then that he was suffocating her, blowing into her mouth and nose so she could not catch a breath. I knew all too well that feeling of not being able to breathe from the many times he'd suffocated me, and it suddenly hit me that she could have died.

* * *

Thankfully, I cannot remember the extent of the violence we encountered in Sanjanah's first year. I know now that when experiences are so traumatic and overwhelming, the brain often hides the memories to protect a person from the emotional pain of recalling the events. As a result, I do not remember much from Sanjanah's first year of life, and I still feel sad about this.

I do remember a time when Mum wanted to treat me to a haircut and colour. Dion had cut and dyed my hair when I was pregnant with Janaya and he did a good job but I had not had my hair done at a salon since. I wanted to take Mum up on her offer so begged and reasoned with Dion. He eventually agreed, and I had my hair restyled with blonde streaks through it. It took just under three hours, and I returned home feeling brand new. I wondered if Dion would like my new look. I found out when I walked in the house and shut the front door behind me. Dion punched me on the side of my head. I hadn't expected it so had not braced myself for impact. Pain seared from my head into my neck, settling into a sharp throbbing as he shouted at me: "Who have you been with? What's his name?"

"I was at the hairdressers," I replied.

"Do you think I'm stupid? It doesn't take three hours to get your hair done! Who is he?" he persisted.

"I just got my hair done then came straight back home."

"It took three hours and you look even uglier than before you left?"

This continued for hours—accusations, insults, punches and slaps. I decided I would never have my hair done in a salon again.

* * *

We had regular 'family group conferences' with social workers, lawyers, counsellors, Mum and Dad, and Dion's parents. They asked Dion to take a drug test. I was not smoking dope anymore, so he made me pee into a container beforehand which he put in his pocket and took with him. He went to the toilet and poured my urine into the sample cup. The test came back negative for drugs and the social worker made everyone clap for him at the next meeting.

Dion told me before each meeting what I was allowed to say. He threatened to beat me and my parents if I said anything that departed from the script.

At one conference prior to Sanjanah's birth, my dad read out a letter he had written from the viewpoint of Janaya as an older child, a child raised without her mother, a child whose mother had been murdered by her father. It was a beautifully written and well-articulated letter, but it was confronting. Dad broke down in tears and sobbed as he read. I looked at the floor. I couldn't bear to see him cry. I had rarely seen my father cry, maybe only once years ago when his dad passed away. Hearing my dad so distraught broke something deep inside me. My sister, Melissa, was there too, and out of the corner of my eye I saw her wiping away tears. My mum looked so broken and frail. A lump grew in my throat, but I fought back my own tears. Dion's continual mocking and mimicking of me as I cried had hardened me. Crying was a weakness. I didn't like people to see me cry or show any emotion at all.

Throughout the years I was with Dion, Mum and Dad never gave up hope. They never stopped loving me. They had no idea of the details or the extent of what went on behind closed doors, but they definitely knew I was being abused. Mum actually ended up in the hospital due to the stress of the situation, not being able to help me, and dealing with child protection services and lawyers. Dad lost himself in it all. He kept books full of notes about times he saw me and wrote down everything I said, word for word. He did the same whenever he spoke on the phone to social workers and lawyers. It took its toll on both of them, but they never gave up on me. I found out later on that they had planned to put me on a plane and send me to family in Australia to get me away from Dion. They even got me a passport. I have no recollection of having the passport photo taken, but when I saw the passport photo years later, I looked like death. I was so gaunt, so pale, and my eyes were black and sunken.

My sister, Melissa, once tried to help me escape out a bedroom window, but Dion walked in as I was halfway out and managed to persuade me to stay. I have no recollection of this event but I am so grateful that throughout the years my family continued to love and care about me.

* * *

I will never forget the events of Mother's Day 2001. Mum and Dad popped around for a visit after dropping Janaya off at Dion's parents for the morning. His parents would then drop her off at our place later that afternoon. Dion became irate as soon as he saw my parents pull up at our house. "What are they doing here?" he shouted. "They'd better be gone before Janaya comes."

After Mum and Dad left, Dion came into the lounge and turned off the TV. He glared at me and said, "I'm going to make your Mother's Day miserable." He wouldn't let me move off the couch until Janaya arrived. If I tried to get up, he'd just shove me back down, yelling at me. When his parents arrived, he sent me straight to the bedroom. I came out after they'd left but he wouldn't let me anywhere near Janaya. He put her in our bedroom and told her to stay there.

Janaya was shut in the room for almost an hour while Dion assaulted me. Sanjanah was awake and crying to be picked up, but I couldn't get to her either. When the beating eventually ended and he allowed me to go and get my babies, I found little Janaya sitting on the edge of the bed, her legs dangling, hands clasped together in her lap, staring blankly at the floor. She hadn't moved the entire time. My heart broke for her.

I wanted out. I'd had enough. I had to get away, but I didn't know how. It felt like the violence was never going to end, and there were moments I feared for my life. The abuse was non-stop, and seeing Janaya so dejected was the final catalyst. I decided I was going to leave him one way or another. I wanted to find a solution at the upcoming family conference, but Dion was adamant about what I could and couldn't say.

After days of torment, Mum and Dad came to visit. This was my opportunity. I shut the lounge door as Dion instructed so he could listen without being in the room. I spoke to my parents as if everything was fine. I couldn't let Dion hear me say anything against him, but as we talked, I grabbed a pen and paper. I hesitated because I knew if I wrote on that piece of paper, my decision to leave was final, and I feared Dion would follow through on his threats to kill me and my family. I was terrified I was signing my loved ones' death warrants, but I knew I could not go on with Dion. Opportunities to get free were few and far between, so I scribbled the note to Mum and Dad and gestured to them not to read it until they were in the car. I wrote:

"Can you call the police and tell them to come around at about one o'clock so Dion doesn't know I told you to ring them? Tell them to take him straight out to the car and get him out of my way. He's been beating me up the last three days 'cos he wants me to lie at the meeting and I said I won't 'cos I'm sick of him getting away with it. He said if I leave him, he'll hunt me down and kill me, and he'll kill you two and Melissa, Brigitta and Ingrid. He's got it all planned. He's got his mates to help him. I'll ring you this afternoon."

I hoped any retaliation from Dion would be against me and not my parents, but I wanted them to know about the threats he had made towards them and my sisters so they could decide whether to run the risk. I thought we would all need to go into hiding.

It was simply a waiting game after Mum and Dad left. I had to survive only another couple of hours. It was an anxious wait for that knock on the door and when it finally came, I was dizzy and weak with fear and trepidation.

The police had a great ploy to delude Dion. They told us that my sister's house had been burgled and they needed to question me as I could have information that might aid their investigation. Dion said we would not go with them but would walk to the police station ourselves. I was terrified that he would not allow me to go but when the police looked at me for confirmation I nodded. I was relieved when Dion walked us around the corner to the police station as he said he would. The officer took Sanjanah and I into a room while Dion stayed in the waiting room.

Part of me felt bad for Dion as he sat outside with no clue as to what was going on. Little did he know I was finally confiding in someone about the years of violence, and that I was leaving him. Dion was arrested that day. He spent the night in jail and was released to await his court appearance. In the meantime, a protection order was put in place, specifying Dion was not to come within a certain distance of the girls and me. Dad cleared all my belongings from the house and put them into storage at my uncle's place. Sanjanah and I went to live with Mum, Dad and Janaya. I was twenty years old and Dion was twenty-six. Janaya was almost three, and Sanjanah was nearly one.

* * *

I missed Dion so much after I left. Funnily enough, I loved him despite the horrific abuse. I called Dion when Mum and Dad were out, but somehow they figured it out and hid the phone whenever they left the house.

Perhaps my imagination worked against me. I heard about a rural boot camp, and I imagined Dion going on this and returning a transformed, better man. No more anger, no more abuse. We would be the perfect, loving family I'd always wanted. During the court case, I even raised this idea in my statement to the judge. In response, the judge spoke to me directly. "In my experience," he said, "a leopard never changes its spots."

Even so, the judge gave Dion a suspended sentence. Looking back, this makes no sense to me. After years of abuse towards me and our infant daughters, and with the death threats he made, this suspended sentence could have provided Dion with an opportunity to fulfil those promises before being sent away. It seems even more insane when I recently learned that half of all 'intimate partner violence' deaths in New Zealand occur at a time of actual or intended separation.

Child protection services and the family court offered Dion supervised access with his daughters, but he refused, saying he wanted to see them in his own home and didn't want to be chaperoned. There was no way that was going to happen.

5

The Party Years

My eyes shot open. At least I thought they were open. It was impossible to tell as the room was pitch black, and the absence of light deprived me of my senses. I couldn't see my hands in front of my face. Where was I? How did I get here? I'd consumed a vast amount of alcohol the night before and knew I was going to vomit. I scrambled out of bed, feeling my way along the wall to find a door. I was disoriented, the room was spinning, the floor tilted under my feet, and my need to find a toilet in a hurry made me panic.

I found myself in a wardrobe, not a good place to expel the contents of my stomach. Flustered and frightened, I found a door that led into a hallway, then feeling my way along the wall, opened a door to what I hoped was the bathroom on the other side. Luck was not on my side as I staggered into Brigitta and her boyfriend's room. They were startled. "Oh Keren!" they exclaimed. "Are you okay? Do you need the toilet?"

Brigitta's boyfriend helped me to the bathroom. I don't know how long I spent in there with my head hanging over the white porcelain altar as I vomited, or sprawled on the floor. Finding my way back to the bedroom was another mammoth struggle in the dark. No sooner had I fallen into bed when my mouth filled with the tell-tale saliva again. This time I didn't make it out of the bedroom.

* * *

This was the messy aftermath of a party my sisters threw to celebrate my freedom after leaving Dion. You couldn't see the top of the kitchen table; it was covered by bottles of beer, wine and spirits. I'd never seen anything like it. I was twenty, and this was my first time drinking with anyone besides Dion. I had no clue about the potential repercussions of mixing drinks, so I just went for it! Brigitta's boyfriend at the time did Axl Rose impressions as *Guns N' Roses* blasted on the stereo. It was all totally foreign to me, but I was excited by the fun and freedom, and relished spending time with my sisters after so many years. No one was controlling my every move or word.

I'd spent the previous four and a half years locked away without the freedom to walk around inside my own home let alone venture outside the four walls of my 'prison'. That night, as the drinks kept coming and we made our way into town, I found myself telling complete strangers about the abuse I'd endured and escaped. I thought these men were so friendly as they leaned in close to hear the tales I slurred in my drunken state. I was so naïve. It was, after all, the first time I'd been in a pub. I lost no time in making up for my lost teenage years. After years of abuse, I had developed a warped understanding of the world and had little idea of how to function well within it.

It was Brigitta who helped me get back into more normal activities. She took the girls and I on outings to the pools. We accompanied her to the beach where she fished while her dog raced up and down the shoreline and the girls and I splashed at the edge of the water, playing chicken with the rippling waves as they ebbed in and out.

One day, Brigitta said, "I've got a friend you'd get on really well with. I call her the F-Lady."

"Why do you call her that?" I asked.

"You'll see," she said, laughing.

I was living at Mum and Dad's at the time, and Brigitta had arranged for the F-Lady to pick me up from the farm and take me to the pub. I was so nervous, plagued with worry that she had been persuaded to take her friend's baby sister to the pub out of pity. I was sure that as soon as she saw my pasty white skin, crooked teeth, complete lack of social skills, and what I felt to be my repulsive physical appearance, she would instantly regret agreeing to spend time with me.

Over time, Tania became one of my most precious friends. She was the epitome of cool, naturally beautiful, witty and fun, and I took an instant liking to her. As soon as we left Mum and Dad's that night, I understood her nickname. She *really* liked to use the f-word! It was months before I summoned the courage to ask her real name.

My other dear friend was Naomi. We were introduced by a lady from church who had been mentoring her. Naomi was stunningly beautiful too. Our friendship flourished and we went to church home groups and Bible studies together. We drank and partied a lot as well and would often turn up to church on a Sunday morning reeking of alcohol from the night before.

One night Naomi said we were going to pop in to visit a friend of hers. We drove up Station Road, turned left onto Main Street at the church, right onto Matai Street and about that time I got curious. Could we be going to Tania's? No, that would be too much of a coincidence. Sure enough, we pulled into Tania's driveway.

"Do you know Tania?" I asked.

"Yeah, she's one of my best mates. Do you know her too?"

From then on, the three of us were inseparable. Like my friendship with Tania, I never imagined Naomi and I becoming so close. I felt they were both too awesome, beautiful and popular to want to know me but these two became the best friends I'd ever had. Whenever we were out together, I always felt like the ugly duckling, insecure and socially awkward, but they loved and accepted me.

We spent most Friday and Saturday nights at the bar. We could always find guys who were more than willing to buy us drinks. At first, Tania and Naomi would literally take one arm each and drag me onto the dance floor, but I refused to dance. I gave in eventually and, fuelled by alcohol, forgot that I had no rhythm and couldn't dance to save my life. There I was on the dance floor, drink in one hand, cigarette in the other, feeling like Beyoncé when I probably looked more like a floundering walrus.

One evening Naomi and I met Francis and Patrick, a couple of good-looking brown boys. They bought us drinks and showered us with endless compliments. An R&B love song started playing, and they began dancing and serenading us. They were so smooth and really had the moves. Who wouldn't want to be serenaded by a hot guy who could not only sing but dance as well? Francis danced and sang to me, and by the end of the song I was imagining our babies, what they would look like, and the story we'd tell them about how their dad won my heart, serenading me in a bar. It was like a movie running in my head, a classic tale of boy meets girl.

That was the prelude to my first one-night stand. I'd left Dion months ago, and even though we were well and truly over I felt like I was cheating on him with Francis. Dion was the first and only person I'd ever kissed, the only man I'd made love to, and the father of my babies. I had never imagined sleeping with more than one man in my lifetime because I had always believed he would be the one I'd spend the rest of my life with.

The concept of a one-night stand felt wrong to me. I couldn't fathom being so intimate with someone and then never seeing them again. It felt heartless and empty. I was certain the night with Francis would be the start of something great but I was mistaken. I never saw him again after that night. I felt used and dirty. I decided perhaps Dion was right when he told me no one would ever want me for anything more than sex. I wished I was brown, beautiful, with a perfect smile and figure. Then maybe Francis would've wanted to see me again.

I slept with more than twenty guys over the next two years. Sometimes these were one-night stands; other times it was a 'friends with benefits' relationship that I always hoped would develop into something more meaningful. I also had a number of short-term relationships, none of which lasted much more than a month or two, along with rapes that I never reported because I blamed myself for getting into those situations and not fighting back enough. In some twisted way I felt grateful that these 'men' wanted to touch me at all.

My heart shattered, piece by piece, when I knew I would not see someone again, or I'd run into the guy at a party the following night with the girlfriend he swore he'd broken up with, or I'd see the man with a new girl and he'd pretend not to know me. I felt dirty and unlovable. I despised myself for being so unattractive and for allowing so many men to use me, men who never intended to love me the way I needed to be loved.

All I wanted was to be someone's someone, the person they searched out when they entered a room full of people, the one who made them smile when their eyes found mine. I wanted a man who could make me feel loved and safe. I wanted the fairy tale I'd dreamed of as a child.

* * *

I longed to be independent, to move out of Mum and Dad's, get my own place, and set up a home for just me and the girls. I got a house on Stewart Street and was allowed to have both my daughters living with me. At the time, however, I was seeing Mark. He lived a few blocks away but spent most nights at my home. He brought his friends over and they invited their mates, who brought their mates, and it wasn't long before my house became a hive of activity. Most of the females who visited were fourteen or fifteen years old. They wagged school and came to my house to hang out, listen to music and drink. Most of the males were older teenagers. I knew this wasn't a good environment for my daughters, but several of the teens called me 'Mum' and accepted me in a way I hadn't been before. I liked that.

We drank a lot in that house. The child protection services warned me about my living situation, saying they would uplift the children if things didn't improve. I was determined to sort out my life for my babies. They were the best part of me, and I did not want to lose them again.

I began turning people away, which was hard because these people accepted me. My landlord received complaints when I put an oversized note on my front door with 'SEX' written in bold lettering that was clearly visible to passers-by. Underneath, in smaller lettering, I'd written, "Now that I have your attention, my lawyer has advised me that if I keep having a house full of people, I will lose my girls. I don't mean to be rude but my daughters come first and this is not a drop-in centre."

The note had little effect other than gathering complaints and accusations from the public who thought I was running a brothel. I'd lock my doors at night only to wake each morning to find the lounge packed with people watching cartoons. My attempts to make my house into a family home failed. It remained a drop-in centre for young people to hang out, get drunk and have sex.

Child services made good on their threat. One day, social workers took Janaya and Sanjanah to Mum and Dad. I cried for days. I was solely to blame, and despised myself for being meek and accepting rather than standing up for my children and sending these people away.

After losing my daughters, I drank and partied even more to numb the pain of my messed-up life, family and dreams. I was lost and out of control, an empty shell, desperate for love and acceptance. I lost entire days in the blur of inebriation. On the rare occasion I took the odd puff or two on a friend's joint, the dope and alcohol combination made me fall asleep and not wake for hours.

Many of my male friends had Nazi flags and swastikas on their bedroom walls. They idolised movies like *American History X* and death metal bands like *Cannibal Corpse,* whose music to me sounded and felt unsettlingly demonic. They loved that I was of German heritage, but for all the wrong reasons. A few of these guys were Māori, and their skinhead mentality confused me. They'd go into town late at night and beat up brown boys. One night they dragged a guy back to my front lawn and kicked him with their steel-capped boots. He'd done nothing wrong—he was simply taking a beating because of his skin colour, and I leapt into the middle to try and stop it.

In spite of all this I still enjoyed the company of these people. They were protective and never hurt me. Once, when Dion's young cousin called over my fence saying he was going to tell Dion where I lived, I panicked, and within minutes my friends were there with baseball bats, metal pipes, steel-capped boots and knuckle-busters, ready to take Dion on if he turned up. He didn't.

Although I felt they would never hurt me, they did not, however, respect my home. They would draw racist and satanic symbols on my furniture, and punch and head-butt holes in my walls.

Another night I was with my latest man. Adam was a smooth talking, bandanna-wearing, forestry worker. I was infatuated with him but he only wanted our relationship to be 'friends with benefits'. This hurt me a lot. I longed for so much more. Adam flirted and slept with me, even taking me away for the weekend to his parents' home in Waiouru, but he wasn't able to give me the love and commitment I wanted and needed.

One night Adam was openly flirting with another girl as I sat right beside him on the couch and the girl sat on his other side. I got up and left the room in tears, pushing past my friend Pete to get through the door. Pete didn't like seeing me so upset, and soon I heard a commotion in the lounge. Seeing Pete had pulled a knife on Adam, I jumped on Pete's back to stop him, and Adam took off. His brother and I went looking for him and eventually found him in bed with yet another girl. I continued messing with him anyway, always hoping he would love me and only me.

We once had a huge bonfire in the backyard which seemed like great fun in our drunken state, especially when bottles started exploding, but we were right in the middle of town and got in a lot of trouble. I was evicted from the house on Stewart Street because of the partying. I moved across town and life calmed down a little.

* * *

For a couple of weeks, some girls had been telling me about a 'hot army guy' in town, and finally, at a party one night, I had the chance to meet him. His name was Gareth, and I was attracted to him right away. To my surprise and delight, the feeling was mutual. Gareth came home with me that night and he stayed. By now, I was twenty-two. Gareth was seventeen but he was the first man to treat me well. It's true what they say about men in uniform—he looked so handsome I had to pinch myself, not quite believing he had chosen to be with me. He was out of my league and yet he made me feel good about myself. The belief that I was ugly was ingrained so deep.

Gareth stayed at the army barracks during the week and came to my place on weekends. Sometimes he surprised me during the week, driving over a hundred kilometres from Waiouru to Marton. I'd have no idea he was coming, and he'd turn up late in the evening with flowers and chocolate. He'd walk in the door and I'd almost burst into tears. He said he was missing me too much; he just had to come and see me, stay the night, and then leave in the early morning hours to return to the barracks before anyone noticed he was gone.

One time, he sneaked me into the barracks. Another time we stayed at a mutual friend's house in Waiouru. It was snowing on this visit, and I sat outside in the snow, happily waiting for him to get back from army training.

Gareth loved his mum, and they had a close relationship. I loved that about him. She was a single mum and he took good care of her. He was great with my daughters too. Janaya and Sanjanah were still living with Mum and Dad. Gareth brought them goodies from the army base, like dozens upon dozens of glow sticks. We once took them to a kite day at Ohakea Airbase, and when the girls ran off, he went after them, carrying them back one under each arm. He was amazingly fit and strong. Once, he ran up the Durie Hill Tower in Whanganui with me on his back. I was terrified but exhilarated.

One of my favourite memories of Gareth is the night he got down on his knees and serenaded me with Lonestar's song, *Amazed.* We talked about moving to the Burnham Army Base together and travelling to Germany to find his dad. It all led me to believe Gareth was the one— until the day he texted to say it was too hard, thinking and worrying about me all the time. He wanted to join the SAS, was training hard, and needed to focus his energy and time on fulfilling his dream. I had not seen this break-up coming and was devastated.

Friends who were visiting at the time tried to console me. All I wanted to do was crawl into bed and cry, but they put me in the car and took me to a twenty-first party that night. I sat in the corner the whole time. I didn't want to be there. When they returned me home, I walked in the front door and found Gareth had left a note and his house key. At the end of his note he'd written, "Don't cry because we are over. Smile because we happened."

I hated myself for going to a party I didn't want to go to. I had missed the opportunity to see him and maybe convince him to stay. Thankfully, I had photos of Gareth and mementos of our time together. I knew Gareth would always have a special place in my heart.

* * *

After Gareth left, I began hanging out with some guys from Mongrel Mob families. They hadn't been initiated into the gang at the time, but they embraced the lifestyle and aspirations of the Mob. The guys came to my house to drink, smoke dope, and party.

One afternoon I was sitting on the doorstep drinking, talking and listening to music with one of these guys. Out of nowhere he looked at me and said, "F—, you're ugly, ay Keren." My heart sank. Those words took me back to the bullying at school and the harsh words Dion had said to me. I can't remember how I reacted, probably said something like a sarcastic, "Well thank you," pretending that I didn't feel like I'd just been stabbed in the chest.

I could not trust these guys to look out for me the way my skinhead mates had. They ripped me off, taking televisions, stereos and video players. One night I had drunk myself into a paralytic state and ended up at one of these Mongrel Mob guy's houses. I was so drunk I couldn't move. I was collapsed in the corner of their front porch where about eight or nine guys were hanging out. They knew I was totally gone and thought it was hilarious. They pushed and shoved me, trying to get me to react but I couldn't even speak. Then I heard one of them say, "Let's sh— on her head!" I freaked out but couldn't do anything. They taunted me for ages, pretending they were going to. They had no respect for me at all. And why should they? I had no respect for what I had become either—a hopeless, disgraceful drunk.

As I lay helpless on that porch that night, I wanted a knight in shining armour to come and rescue me from my squalor, to push through the crowd of boys who were taunting and jeering at me, and to lift me gently in his arms out of that dark corner and carry me away and give me all the love and care I was so desperately craving. I wanted someone to transform my nightmarish life into the fairy tale dream I longed for. I wanted someone to love me back to life.

Guys turned up to my house at all hours of the night for sex. I almost always let them in and gave them what they wanted, hoping that one of them might love me and we'd end up getting married and stay together forever. I wasn't even attracted to every guy I slept with, and I had no criteria or standards. I just wanted someone to love me and didn't care who. Because of the way I looked, I felt I had to settle for whatever I could get.

* * *

My parents and I had shared custody of my children, and I was told I would have to go to counselling if I ever wanted to regain full custody. I was apprehensive at first because I'd had many counsellors over the years. We'd sit and talk, I would go home, and nothing would change. Even so, I agreed to begin counselling sessions at the farm with a man by the name of Peter.

Peter was a Christian. He did not flaunt his beliefs, yet his faith shone through. He discovered that the cause of my issues was a deep-rooted fear of rejection and abandonment. Once we had established this, we were able to begin to work through it. This was new territory for me, and I was on the defensive for some time with Peter before I began to trust him and open up about the years of fear, abuse, loneliness and wrenching heartache.

I hadn't noticed much change in myself until I heard an all too familiar knock on the door. I opened it to find one of my 'friends with benefits' on the doorstep. Accustomed as he was to coming in, he stepped into the doorway. Without even thinking, I stopped him and said, "Not tonight." It was a response he was not expecting. "Are you sure?" he asked. It was clear he thought he was doing me a favour by turning up at my house for random sex. This was such an eye-opener for me that I replied, yes, I was sure, and closed the door in his face. The feeling was one of liberation, and from that night on, I did not allow these 'randoms' to use me anymore.

* * *

In August 2003, I started helping out in my sister's classroom at Marton Junction School. I was twenty-two, and this was my first experience of work. My nephew, Riki, was living with me, and a month after I started working at the school, I got a second job with him, picking asparagus. I was now working two part-time jobs and it felt good to be doing something productive rather than drinking and wasting my life away.

Riki and I were about to start asparagus picking on our first day of work, when a guy jumped over the fence to join us. At first, I thought he was an old friend of mine, and was about to say hi, but when he introduced himself as Geoffrey, I realised he wasn't who I thought he was. A couple of days later, however, Riki and I were getting rides to and from work with him, and within a week or two we had started going out and Geoffrey moved in with us. Geoffrey was just seventeen years old.

Geoffrey and I had many deep and meaningful talks. I told him about my abusive past and he told me how his dad left and never acknowledged him in any way. He hated his father and swore he would never abandon his own kids as his dad had done. I liked that he looked up to his uncle, however, who had taught him the value of hard work.

After a couple of months, Geoffrey asked me to move out to his mum's. She had a sleep-out we could stay in. I liked the idea. There was still a constant stream of people turning up at my house, and I figured this was a chance for a fresh start. After all, he must love me if he asked me to move in with him, right?

We had lived together a few weeks when Geoffrey said he was moving to another town to work on a dairy farm. He said he would come and see me a few times a week. After asking me to live with him, I was left all alone. It was awkward around his family. I felt abandoned.

* * *

At the beginning of the following year, I was overjoyed to find out I was pregnant again. Geoffrey had reassured me he would be there for any children he fathered, as he did not want to follow the footsteps of his own dad, but when I told him, he was quiet. My joy at the pregnancy began to dissipate into thin air. There was no excited hug, no tears of happiness at the thought of becoming a dad, and he left that evening leaving me puzzled by his lukewarm reaction to my news.

Over the following weeks, his visits home became fewer, and one evening he called to tell me to get an abortion. I was shattered. Shocked to the core and unable to speak, I hung up the phone. I must have been sobbing and had tears on my face, trying to get out of the lounge and back to the sleep-out, because Geoffrey's mother stopped me and gave me a hug. She sat me down in the house as I gave way to an endless supply of tears.

I was in disbelief over Geoffrey's words. I wanted to curl up in bed and hide, wishing I could go to Mum and Dad's to hug Janaya and Sanjanah, but they were all holidaying in Fiji.

I was pregnant and alone. Abortion was murder. There was no way I could countenance the thought, and the fact that my baby's father wanted me to abort made me feel physically ill. I loved this baby in my belly with a mother's fierceness, just as I had my other two children, and I vowed to protect this precious, innocent life with every ounce of my being.

Geoffrey's visits became less frequent. I hadn't seen him for weeks when he broke up with me. I was about five months pregnant and found out he had a new girlfriend living with him out where he worked. I also discovered he was smoking dope. As far as I know he hadn't been using when we were together, but soon his addiction took over.

When Mum and Dad and my babies returned from Fiji, I spent a lot of time on the farm with them. Five-year-old Janaya and three-year-old Sanjanah were very excited about having a new baby in the family. If the baby was a boy, Sanjanah wanted to name him Clifford the Dog, and if a girl she wanted to name her Dorothy the Dinosaur.

After a while I took all my belongings from Geoffrey's family home and moved into town to prepare for the birth of my third baby. I returned to the same house where I'd once lived with Dion. It was eerie to see the damaged doorframe in the bathroom where Dion had kicked the door in, and the keyholes in all the doors which he had once used to lock the babies and I away. I was determined to make happy memories in this home which had once been a place of horrendous abuse and fear.

Geoffrey and his mum came to visit me there, but all Geoffrey talked about was his new girlfriend, even though here I was, heavily pregnant with his child. The hurt was deep, the sense of loneliness and abandonment intense. Perhaps the counselling was having some effect. Normally I'd be out looking for the next boyfriend. This time, I simply felt disappointment.

* * *

My beautiful third daughter was born on a Wednesday in the Whanganui Hospital. I was twenty-three. I named my blonde-haired, blue-eyed girl Ahnaliyah. My mum and Geoffrey's were with me in labour, but Geoffrey showed no interest. Childbirth is miraculous, and his daughter was about to enter the world, and he was in the waiting room, texting his girlfriend.

The pushing stage was intense and I knew she was close. I asked where Geoffrey was, and his mum brought him in for the birth. She was placed in my arms, and I couldn't believe my eyes as I looked down on another perfectly beautiful, angelic baby. Her striking blue eyes looked into mine, and I was mesmerized. I ran my fingers across her buttery soft face, and reached down to touch her hand and admire her tiny, perfectly formed fingers. She immediately wrapped her fingers around mine. I was overwhelmed with love for this precious baby girl.

Mum and Geoffrey's mum took turns cuddling my baby, and Geoffrey's mum offered her son a cuddle. "Isn't she beautiful?" she asked, but Geoffrey refused to hold her. "It's just a baby," he said, and left the room. The midwife was disgusted with his behaviour and I cried because a part of me hoped when he laid eyes on his daughter, he would become the doting dad I dreamed he would be and I would have the happy family I longed for.

I cradled my precious baby in my arms, overwhelmed with love, but sad because her father had rejected her. I couldn't understand how he could walk away from such a perfect baby, his own flesh and blood. I vowed to give her all the love she needed.

* * *

At a recent family conference, everyone had agreed that the children should be returned to my care following Ahnaliyah's birth, and were even prepared to go to court to speak on my behalf. Peter, my counsellor, agreed to write a letter of support.

In preparation, I had moved into my home, and with money I saved from the benefit, bought new furniture and had the house set up for the arrival of my new baby, and with the hope of Janaya and Sanjanah coming home.

Now that Ahnaliyah was born, Janaya and Sanjanah started gradually transitioning back into my care. For the first time in six years, I could see my babies every day. We were all together, the four of us under the same roof.

As I stood in their doorways watching them sleep each night, my heart was so full. I adored these three precious girls so much that it hurt physically. I was in awe that I'd created such beautiful children. I wondered who they would grow up to be and what God had planned for their lives. I wanted a far better life for them than I'd had. Regret felt like a sack of rocks on my back. I knew my compromises had exposed my babies to dysfunction in their formative years. In my own dysfunction I had failed to protect them, and a self-imposed guilty verdict oppressed me like a dark cloud. They were my entire world, and my love for them was overwhelming.

* * *

I applied for sole custody of my children. Dion and Geoffrey received their court summons for the hearing so they could dispute my application if they wanted, but neither showed up, so my request was granted. The relief was indescribable. My babies were back. We were finally a family. It was time to create the loving home I'd always wished for, and to build precious memories together.

For years, my life had been filled with darkness and pain. I hit rock bottom then was engulfed by the quicksand at the bed of the pit. I'd been used and abused. My heart was broken, wounded and bleeding. I had tried to wrap up the gaping, oozing wounds in my soul with a filthy, germ-infected bandage of alcohol and looking for love in all the wrong places. I was an empty shell, devoid of identity and any sense of worth.

It was time to start over and change the trajectory of our lives...

6

Homecoming

Anyone who belongs to Christ has become a new person.
The old life is gone; a new life has begun!

2 Corinthians 5:17, NLT

The return of my babies sparked a flame within me. I felt alive again. I had something precious to live for. They gave me the will to pick myself up and carry on.

I started going to church again in early 2004 when I was pregnant with Ahnaliyah. Mum, Dad and the girls would pick me up from Geoffrey's mums on their way to church. I was apprehensive at first, worried that I might be judged for the lifestyle I'd been leading and the fact that I was once again pregnant out of wedlock. This was not the case at all. I was embraced with a rapturous welcome home. I found out that people had been praying for me the whole time I was gone, praying that I'd return to Jesus and to the plan He had for my life. I was greeted with warmth and love.

After moving into my own home with my daughters, I began going to church on a weekly basis. I also started going to prayer meetings, home groups, and Bible studies. I felt as if I was home. I felt safe. When I brought Ahnaliyah home from hospital, people from the church came by with meals. When I was sick with the flu, they brought me soup. I felt God's love filtering into my life by way of the thoughtfulness and generosity of others. I was humbled by the support and kindness people showed me. Accustomed as I was to physical, mental, and emotional abuse, the genuine kindness and friendship offered was new to me, and I was not sure how to receive it.

* * *

Even as a small child I was fascinated by the supernatural. Prophecy, tongues, healing—all these things were part of our everyday lives. I was inspired by my parents and people in the church who heard God speak, not just for themselves, but for others as well. I longed to hear God's voice for myself but all my prayers and conversations until now had seemed one-sided. During my time with Dion, I remember crying out to God as I was beaten, but my prayers seemed to dissipate into the atmosphere. *Where is God in all this?* I wondered.

The first time I clearly heard from God was in 2004. It wasn't an audible voice, but I knew beyond a shadow of a doubt that it was Him. I can't explain how I knew. No earthly words can accurately describe it unless you experience the presence of God for yourself. Phrases replayed over and over in my mind. They seemed vaguely familiar, but I had no idea what they meant. After several days I figured out the words were from a song by *The Pretenders* called *I'll Stand by You*. My favourite music was R&B and hip-hop, so this song was not one I knew but after learning the lyrics, I saw how relevant they are to God's love and promises.

The realisation that God had spoken to me blew my mind. The words meant so much to me and were like salve to the oozing wounds in my heart. A peace flowed through the deepest, darkest recesses of my brokenness. I felt loved and my spirit felt brand new.

I could feel God knocking at the door of my heart. His love for me was tangible, and it wasn't long before I made a conscious decision to live for Him.

I wrote a letter to my pastor and his wife, Phil and Lisa Dent, to let them know what was going on in my heart, and they led me through the Sinner's Prayer. I was born again, forgiven, my past was no longer held against me. As the months passed, many people commented on the dramatic change they saw in my outer appearance.

Phil and Lisa loved and discipled me, being there for me, teaching, listening, supporting and praying for me. They encouraged me to do a Bible study course which covered the basic principles of Christianity. The content was nothing new. I'd learned it all as a child growing up in church, but something resonated deeper in my spirit this time. After doing the section on baptism, I understood what it meant to be baptised. Being submerged under the water would symbolise my old life was dead and buried. Coming up out of the water would symbolise me rising to my new life of faith in Jesus. I was eager to take this next step.

I was baptised on the 14th of August 2005. I was twenty-four. I had written my testimony and this was handed to people as they entered the church that morning. I wanted people to know my story so they could understand the transformative work God had performed in my life.

Dad and Pastor Phil baptised me, and as I came up out of the water, my church family sang the song I'd requested, *Come Holy Spirit*. The plea for the Holy Spirit to fill me and fall in fresh ways upon me was my heart's cry. Whenever I sing that song now, I can feel the Holy Spirit wrap me in love.

Many of my church family had words from God for me the morning of my baptism. Pastor Phil was praying for me and sensed

God's pleasure over me that day. He described God jumping with joy and smiling as I took this significant step in my faith. Standing in front of the church he spoke to me:

"Just as a natural diamond is formed in darkness and under intense and immense pressure, so you have been formed in darkness. Once a diamond is mined, its appearance belies the inward beauty. It looks unattractive and even insignificant. To the untrained eye it would be thrown away as a simple rock. Yet from that point on, as the master jeweller begins his work on that rock, the new shape begins to emerge and the beauty hidden within is being formed. In the times of pressure and heat, it starts to be revealed. The jeweller sets to cutting off and removing the outer layers of the rock. He cuts and chisels, taking away the outer layers of dirt and rock. Then the process continues with grinding and shaping. Finally, the master jeweller polishes the perfectly-formed diamond so every surface reflects the light that is shone upon it, and the diamond almost appears as if the light itself comes from within.

This is the journey of your life. There have been times of great darkness, extreme pressure, and heat. That which the enemy has sought to use to bring death and destruction, God has and will use for good. As you continue to surrender your life and allow the Master to chip away and remove that which is from the old, you will begin to see a radiant beauty revealed from within. Yes, it is already there, that beauty. It has been there from the beginning; it has just been hidden by other things. The real you is slowly but surely going to shine out from your life and who you are. Just like the diamond, the beauty was hidden by the outer shell. God will lovingly and carefully remove the outer shell. At times it will hurt. There will come more trials. The tests will come, but all you need to do is trust Him. Give yourself whole-heartedly to Him, and you will be amazed what God will do through and in your life, and through the lives of those who are near and dear to you.

God wants to encourage you today, Keren, that there is much more to come. The best is yet to come for you. But know this, there will be tests. There will be trials. God doesn't want to hide that from you. He wants you to know so you can go in with your eyes open. But He will be with you. He wants you to lean on Him. Trust Him. Trust Him with all your heart. He will be your strength. He will be your guide. And God will be there, as He has been from the start."

* * *

I developed an insatiable desire to study the Bible. I was hungry for knowledge. My Bible was always open on the dining room table, and I continually rushed back to it throughout the day. I had a keen interest in theology, particularly Eschatology. My fascination with the End Times was immense. I read countless books and listened to many teachings about End Time prophecies. I studied different interpretations and ideas about the rapture—whether there was a rapture at all, and if so, will it take place pre-tribulation, mid-tribulation or post-tribulation. I tried desperately to construct a timeline in relation to the possible rapture, the rise of the anti-Christ, the tribulation, the second coming, and the millennial reign of Jesus.

I was so excited about Jesus returning that I made huge posters and hung them in the front windows of my house. They said *Maranatha,* meaning 'The Lord is coming'. My heart was enraptured by the renewed assurance and hope that Heaven was my true home. The excitement that Jesus would return to earth for us one day was intoxicating. Our life on earth is miniscule in comparison to eternity. Earth is not home, Heaven is.

I was also interested in learning about Christian persecution. I signed up to receive the *Voice of the Martyrs* magazines and my heart broke for Christians around the world who were being (and continue to be) imprisoned, tortured and murdered for their faith. I learned how Jesus' disciples were brutally tortured and killed. Peter and Andrew were crucified, James the son of Zebedee was beheaded,

Thomas was speared to death, Matthew was stabbed to death, James the son of Alphaeus was stoned and clubbed to death, and tradition holds that John was plunged into boiling oil (according to Tertullian, everyone in the audience in the Colosseum converted to Christianity upon witnessing his miraculous escape).

I was deeply shocked yet encouraged by the stories I read in DC Talk's book, *Jesus Freaks,* which detailed accounts of the martyrdom of dozens of believers, young and old, throughout the centuries. They could have escaped their horrific torture and deaths if they denounced Jesus, but they praised God in the face of pain and death. Many sang hymns as they were being burned or beaten. This tremendous strength to continue to love, obey and praise God in the worst circumstances filled me with unshakable faith.

I looked into why I believed what I believed and was fascinated by what I found. I wasn't satisfied to merely believe just because that was all I'd ever known, or just because my family believed. I didn't want my Christianity to simply be out of tradition or sentimentality. I studied and uncovered a wealth of historical evidence which supported Jesus and His resurrection.

Dad shared my love for study and the scriptures, and he was keen to engage with me in studying and discussing the ways of God. It was a precious time of reconnecting with Dad. One of his favourite scriptures was the story of the Bereans in Acts 17:

> *They received the message with great eagerness*
> *and examined the Scriptures every day to see if*
> *what Paul said was true (v 11, NIV).*

I asked Dad a lot of questions, and it became evident that our thought processes were extremely similar. The questions I raised were the same as many he'd asked his own father. This was remarkable to me. My dad was a wise and thoughtful man, and the idea that I was following in his footsteps filled me with such pride and zeal. If Dad didn't have an answer for me, he'd be honest and say so rather than pretend to know. I respected this about him. We would then study and search for the answer together.

Dad and I also bonded through attending conferences and healing meetings together. I couldn't get enough of soaking in the presence and anointing of God, and in these environments I found myself more and more convinced of God and His perfect love for me. My spirit came alive and God began a transformative healing in my life.

The Lord is close to all whose hearts are crushed by pain,
and he is always ready to restore the repentant one.

Psalm 34:18, TPT

One particular healing meeting remains strong in my memories. Dad and I went along together. I was believing for a miracle that night. My faith was so strong—I believed that the two tattoos of Dion's name would miraculously disappear. I knew that nothing was impossible for God, that erasing ink marks in the skin was easy for Him. When I went forward to receive prayer, the healing evangelist was touched deeply by my faith. He covered the tattoos with his hands and prayed. As soon as he finished praying, I opened my eyes and looked down at my wrist. The tattoo was still there. Looking me in the eye, the evangelist told me that God does not always work the way we expect Him to, but he also told me that God had shown him that the tattoos would be gone before Christmas. Each morning after that I woke up believing the tattoos would have disappeared, and each morning I was disappointed. But God never goes back on His promises, and just a few weeks before Christmas I had my tattoos surgically removed. God may not always answer our prayers in the way we expect, but He does answer prayers in His own way, in His own time.

There was a Christian bookstore in Marton, run by a lovely couple. I loved visiting this store. It had such a peaceful atmosphere. I was there every week hiring out Christian videos. Preachers such as Jesse Duplantis and Joyce Meyer were instrumental in my new life with Jesus. Jesse Duplantis' accounts of his personal heavenly encounters opened my mind and heart to God's desire to make Himself known to mankind and His sovereignty to let us see into the spiritual realm. I longed to experience similar encounters.

During the years I spent drinking and partying, I never doubted God's existence. My philosophy became, "So what if I drink? So what if I smoke? So what if I sleep around? I haven't murdered anyone." I talked myself into it as a way of justifying my lifestyle because deep down I knew the life I was leading was wrong.

I chose to believe I wasn't hurting anyone. I hadn't murdered anyone. I wasn't a criminal. I wasn't breaking any laws ... but I was. I was breaking God's laws. Now I wanted everyone to experience His love, grace and forgiveness the way I had. I told God I would do whatever He wanted me to do, go wherever He wanted me to go. I wanted to be His hands, His feet, and His mouthpiece on earth, a walking, talking billboard for Jesus.

* * *

One day in September 2006, a lady in church relayed a message to me that came directly from God. I was humbled and awed when she stood in front of the congregation and said:

"God has spoken to me five times this week about you. He gave me four pictures, one after the other. In the first one I couldn't hear anything but I could see. You were sitting on grass with children the age of your children now, and you were communicating with them and teaching them. You had those children in the palm of your hand. You were speaking life into these kids, Keren. And the Lord says, 'This is the gift I've given you.' And He wants you to rise up in it.

In the next picture I saw school children. They wore uniforms and were all around you. *You were speaking to them and they were listening to what you were saying. Once again, you were speaking life into them. Their eyes were fixed on you, Keren. You had something to give.*

The picture changed again. The children were young teenagers, fourteen or fifteen-ish, and you were on the street. They were all around you, and you were walking and talking to them. Again, they were listening intently to what you had to offer. You have something within you—you have God within you, you have the Holy Spirit within you. God wants you to start bringing it out and impacting people. These children were listening to you. You have something they need to hear.

The picture changed again and this time it was young mothers with babies. I saw prams. It looked like somewhere outside a building—I don't know where. You were mixing amongst them. Two of the mothers pointed at you and made their way to you. And people were coming to you from all over the place. They were pointing you out Keren, you! And the Lord wants to say to you, 'Rise up in the giftings and callings that I have for you,' because there is a seed that has been planted. I know that you have a natural desire to study, and God says, 'That is a desire that I have planted within you,' and the Lord wants you to know, 'Start to rise up and grasp that which I have given you.'

The Lord loves you, Keren. He wants to encourage you. God sees you differently to how you see yourself, I'm really aware of that.

God reminds me through all of this that I couldn't hear what you were saying to any of these children and young people, these mothers, but I didn't need to because I could see that God was within you. You were radiating His love, and you were impacting them. It was so powerful. He showed it to me four or five times over the week, so I understood it was important that I had to tell you now."

Elation coursed through my veins. The God who created the universe cared enough for me to get this message to me, to give me hope for, and insight into, my future. At the time I couldn't have known that years later, this prophecy was partially fulfilled when I worked closely with children in my own home and also with caregivers and children through my church playgroup.

* * *

In 2007, I started working as the church treasurer, counting and banking tithes, balancing the books, and co-signing cheques. I also served as a Children's Church leader. Janaya and Sanjanah still remember a couple of the lessons I taught. To illustrate the story about the 'Woman at the Well' in John 4:4-42, I brought in an ornamental well from Dad's garden and had the children re-enact the story. When learning about the Shield of Faith in Ephesians 6:16, I made up a cardboard shield and had a child hold it up to 'defend' themselves from the Enemy's ammunition in the form of balled-up socks thrown by the other children. I also helped in the crèche and was in charge of stocktaking.

Around this time, I started working at a local motel. I was the relief manager while the manager had some much-needed time out to play golf each Saturday. Later I got a third job working as a telemarketer.

Mum and Dad were a great support during this time. I had my hands full as a working single mum with three young children. They looked after the girls while I was at work and whenever I needed a break. They even mowed my lawns, and Dad did maintenance that was needed around the house. I was so grateful to have such loving parents who were always there for me and never gave up on me.

Family life was amazing! I loved being a mum and having my daughters with me. I prayed with the girls every night, and before they went to sleep, I'd tell them I was so glad that Jesus had chosen me to be their mum. Janaya and Sanjanah would say their own little prayers each night too. In my memories box I have a note dated February 2005 which reads:

"This month we started praying together as a family every night before we go to bed. On the first night Janaya, who was six years old, said this lovely prayer…

'*To Jesus. I love you. Thank you for coming to this world and dying on the cross. Thank you for Mum, Sanjanah, Ahnaliyah, Grandma and Grandad. Thank you for a sunny day. Please send us a daddy who loves us and who won't go away. Thank you for lots of people who love us.*'''

What an insightful prayer for such a young child! Still, the part about the daddy who wouldn't go away broke my heart. How I wished they didn't have to grow up without the sort of loving father I had.

Every night I told my girls how much I loved them and how beautiful they were. Eventually they started replying, "We know, Mum. You tell us all the time." Over the years I took them to activities including Mainly Music, playgroups, Every Girls Rally, swimming lessons, music lessons, ballet, and regular children's events at the town library.

I loved getting them ready and off to kindy and school each morning. I put little notes in their lunchboxes telling them how much I loved them and wishing them a good day. I couldn't wait to pick them up each afternoon, and attend their discos, prizegivings, productions, sports days, and pet days.

I had a terrifying experience one afternoon when Mum and I went to pick up the girls from school. We found Janaya right away, but we looked everywhere for Sanjanah and couldn't find her. We even got the principal, teachers, and other students in on the search. She was nowhere on school grounds. I started to panic. I was on the verge of tears. My immediate thought was that Dion had kidnapped my baby. I was an absolute wreck, rushing around checking and re-checking every inch of the school. Eventually we discovered she had gone home with one of her friends. With no communication from her friend's mother, no checking with me, she just took her home for a playdate. I was so shaken by this experience and it took me a long time to get over the shock of thinking my daughter had been taken.

* * *

Every Christmas, the girls and I made a special present for Jesus. We wrote thank-you prayers to acknowledge all the things we were grateful for that year. I printed out photos of fun things we had done, and we made a giant poster with 'Happy Birthday, Jesus' at the top, and a collage of all our prayers and photos. The girls took our finished work to the Christmas service at church, and were called up the front during the service to show everyone their creation. It was a lovely family tradition.

The girls and I had 'mummy-daughter dates' where we spent a whole day of one-on-one time doing whatever they wanted. They always looked forward to these special days.

Twice a year I took Janaya and Sanjanah on shopping sprees for their summer or winter clothing. They loved putting on their new clothes and doing fashion parades once we got home. Often, they dressed up and put on shows for me. Most were based on Bible stories. I loved my girls so much and was so pleased that life was better for us now.

I didn't miss the partying and drama that my previous lifestyle precipitated. This new life was infinitely better. I no longer felt lost and outcast. I felt loved and had renewed hope for my future and that of my children.

I wish I could say that life was perfect after giving my heart to God, that all the pieces miraculously fell into place and all my lifelong dreams came true. But they didn't. At my baptism, Pastor Phil had forewarned me of the trouble and trials that would lie ahead. So had Jesus. He never promised life would be perfect. Christians aren't immune to hardships and trials. John 16:33 (MSG) says, "In this godless world you will continue to experience difficulties. But take heart! I've conquered the world."

7

Waiting in Vain

My nerves were like electricity under my skin. Anxious anticipation would not allow me the luxury of sitting still. I paced around the house like a cat on a hot tin roof so excessively that I risked wearing the carpet bare beneath my feet. I must have checked and reapplied my make-up at least half a dozen times. The clothes all over my bedroom floor attested to the number of times I changed my outfit trying to find the perfect one. I boiled the jug countless times and furtively peeked out the lounge window every minute awaiting his arrival. When his car finally pulled up at my home, the nerves detonated, rendering me lightheaded and weak-kneed, and I seriously considered hiding and pretending I wasn't home.

* * *

The church had gifted me a computer to do their accounts on when I began working as their treasurer. For the first time in my life I had access to the big, wide, and sometimes scary world of the internet. I spent hours reading an endless array of End Times and theology websites, excited by the vast amount of material available at my fingertips. I already had dozens of resources on these subjects, but now I had a seemingly infinite wealth of information in which to lose and immerse myself. I also discovered blogs, and spent way too much time having theological discussions with fellow Christians and atheists from around the world.

I was single for over three and a half years after Geoffrey left. Now that I had a computer, it wasn't long before I signed up to a number of online dating sites in the hope of finding the man I'd dreamed of since childhood, the one God had ordained for me since the beginning of time. I wanted a good Christian man, someone honest, faithful, loving, gentle… someone like my dad. I wanted a man who would love my children as if they were his own and help me teach them about Jesus.

Online dating was relatively new back then, especially to me. The media provided continual reminders of how dangerous online relationships could be, and cited the many violent crimes committed when people did meet up. Mum was concerned and vocal about the possibility of me being misled, harmed or worse.

I wanted to marry someone who shared my beliefs, so I limited my communications to those men who described themselves as Christians. I quickly learned, as I had been warned, that not everyone was who they claimed to be.

It was difficult to determine who was a genuine Christian online, but I usually could tell after a few days of chatting. Those who weren't genuine slipped up eventually, and I'd see the cracks in their conversations.

* * *

It was mid-2007. I was twenty-six and in conversation with two amazing Christian men. Thirty-one-year-old Joachim who lived in

Taranaki, and thirty-five-year-old Mason who lived in Hawke's Bay.

After much prayer and consideration, I chose to pursue a relationship with Mason. It was hard letting Joachim know my decision, but I gave him my friend Kaz's phone number, thinking they might hit it off.

I believed I'd made the right choice with Mason. We chatted online and over the phone for a couple of months before arranging to meet in person that September.

We decided to meet at my house. Mason was arriving from Hastings, and the anticipation of the day of our first meeting was almost too much to bear. Would he take one look at me and wish he hadn't bothered with the hundred-and-sixty-six-kilometre drive? Would he be repulsed by my appearance? Would I be awkward, weird, say the wrong things? He knocked on my door several times before I bit the bullet and decided to open it and let him in.

Our meeting went well despite my nerves. Mason enjoyed looking through the library of End Times books on my bookcase, and we talked at length about the things of God. I couldn't stop smiling as I watched him leave. However, the thought crossed my mind as he drove away that I couldn't imagine myself kissing him. That puzzled me. I put it down to our age difference. Mason was eight-and-a-half years older than me and glaringly different to any other guy I'd ever been with before. But maybe that was exactly what I needed—a mature, strait-laced, gentle and kind Christian man.

Prior to his visit, we agreed we would wait until he returned to Hawke's Bay before saying whether we were keen on each other. I suggested this because I did not want to endure a face-to-face rejection. I knew it would take him two hours to get home, but as soon as his car disappeared around the corner I rushed to my computer and waited on tenterhooks for him to message me.

After what seemed like an eternity, he finally came online. I could see that he was typing. I sat forward in my seat in anticipation of his message. What would he say? Did he enjoy his time in Marton? Did he like me? I braced myself to be turned down. He seemed to be typing for so long. Was he trying to find the gentlest way of telling me he wasn't interested? I was beyond surprised when I read that he loved his time with me, that he was relieved to find I was who I said I was, and that my face matched the photos on my dating profile. He liked me and was keen to continue seeing where things went with us.

We started dating 'officially' in early October 2007. Our nightly phone calls often lasted until the early hours of the morning even though Mason had to be up at three a.m. for work. Our theological discussions were lively and engaging, and I enjoyed hearing stories of his childhood and of the miracles he had experienced in his life.

I placed Mason on a pedestal. I saw him as being a much better Christian than I was, due to my past. So when he confided in me one night on the phone that he saw nothing wrong with drinking alcohol in moderation and that he often enjoyed a glass or two of an evening, I started drinking again. After four years of sobriety, I thought that if he did it, it must be okay.

* * *

I made many trips to Hastings to spend time with Mason, first by bus, but after falling asleep on a stranger's shoulder one too many times, I got a bank loan to buy my very first car, a little white Ford Festiva which affectionately became known as 'the granny-mobile'.

Mason showed me around Hawke's Bay and introduced me to his family and friends. We went together to his nephew's rugby games and taekwondo tournaments, and his niece's netball games. We went to the movies and out for dinner, and many times I drove home in tears after leaving him to return to Marton. I hated the distance between us and missed him whenever we were apart.

That summer, I attended a church barbeque at my friend Kaz's home in Marton. The minute I arrived she came up to me and exclaimed,

"Guess who's here!" I was surprised when she told me that Joachim had travelled from Taranaki to be at the barbeque. I remember thinking that things must be going great between him and Kaz, and I was so happy for them. All I said to him that night was a fleeting, "Hi." I spent the evening outside on the deck with Mum and Dad, while Joachim was inside, I assumed with Kaz. It wasn't until eight years later that I learned he hadn't been there for Kaz at all.

Mason and I bought each other promise rings for our first Valentine's Day together. The rings represented our commitment to each other. Mason compared it to how in movies, high school boys used to give their sweetheart their jacket as a way of showing they were going steady. I was falling in love.

As a born-again Christian, I wanted to do things right this time around and have my 'happily ever after'. Mason and I were firm in our beliefs about waiting for marriage before sleeping together. This was important to me because I wanted to do things God's way to protect our future marriage and make our wedding night special. However, I longed for him to kiss me, and my anticipation grew every time we were together. Each visit I thought, *Will this be the time we share our first kiss?* I returned home after every visit still waiting for that elusive moment, but the thought I'd had when we first met kept ringing in my ears: *I can't imagine kissing him.*

Mason and I talked about relocating me and the girls to Hastings. Mum and Dad didn't like the idea of uprooting our lives and moving across the country, away from family support. They wanted me to wait until I had a ring on my finger before I made such a big decision. Mason said he couldn't propose until I moved there and we'd had more time to get to know each other.

* * *

The move to Hastings was planned for December 2008. Mason and I had been together for about fourteen months, and I began to realise what a huge thing this was for me. I was about to enter a new and exciting, yet terrifying, chapter in my life.

I had been born, raised, and lived, in small town Marton for my entire twenty-eight years, with Mum and Dad just a phone call away. Now I was heading across the country to Hastings where I knew no one. Was I being foolish, going so far to be with a man who had still not even kissed me?

It was Janaya and Sanjanah's last day at South Makirikiri School before our big move. I headed out that morning for a mini-assembly, where the girls would be presented with their leaving certificates. I did not want people to see me upset, so I kept a poker-face even though deep down I was an emotional wreck and questioned the wisdom of this decision that would take my daughters away from all that was familiar. It had taken the girls over three years to form relationships, and both now had very close circles of friends.

As I sat in the car waiting for the bell to ring for the assembly, I watched Sanjanah playing with her friends. They were all over her, almost pulling her arms out of their sockets because they adored her. She had celebrity status! I felt an overwhelming surge of guilt. Why was I taking her away from her friends just when she'd come out of her shell and gained confidence in herself? Was I being selfish? Was I a bad mother, uprooting my babies for a man? I was more fearful for my daughters than for myself, not knowing what the future held for us away from family, friends, and everything we knew.

Both the older girls had farewell parties before we left Marton. By this time, Mum and Dad had sold the family farm and moved into town. We had Sanjanah's party at their home in Bredins Line. She invited five of her little school friends. Her three best friends brought her presents and wrote sweet notes in cards for her. One by one as their parents turned up and they left, her friends gave Sanjanah hugs goodbye. It was heart-breaking.

Janaya's farewell was a pool party with her entire class, hosted by friends from church at their home in Bonny Glen. I bought her a disposable camera so she could take photos of her friends to take to Hastings with her.

On our last Sunday at church, the girls and I were called to the front, and the whole congregation gathered around us. Different people took turns praying for us and prophesying over us. Manny Down told me, "There are going to be times when you're over in Hastings when you're going to wonder if you made the right decision in moving. But God would have you know that He has planned this move for you, and it has been planned since before you were born. He has gone before you and made a way for you."

* * *

Hastings was so big in comparison to Marton. I was always getting lost and having to print out maps before leaving the house. The heat was a huge shock too. Hawke's Bay summers were unbearably hot. I spent a lot of time trying to keep cool sitting on the tiles on the bathroom floor, the only room in the house where I could escape the swelter.

Mason lived about twenty minutes out of Hastings with his mum, and his nephew and niece. Mason and his niece often came to see us in town and the girls always looked forward to their visits. They loved the fact that he wasn't afraid to get down and play with them. It was very endearing, and made me love him even more. Four-year-old Ahnaliyah adored Mason. She told me I wasn't allowed to marry him because she was going to. We enjoyed the endless array of activities Hawke's Bay had to offer—playgrounds, concerts, parades, galas, beaches, rivers, waterfalls, pools, mini-golf and more. We were all loving the new fun-filled lifestyle at home too, with water fights, countless board and card games, and movie-and-munchie nights. Life was good.

We visited a lot of churches in the first few months after we moved to Hastings. I had expected we would end up at the Miracle Centre, since it was an Assembly of God church like the church I was raised in.

However, God had other plans and planted us in Equippers Church. The pastor at the time had a great gifting in the prophetic. I loved seeing the Holy Spirit take over and move in these services.

The girls thrived and settled well into school and kindergarten. Ahnaliyah went to a wonderful Christian preschool and I loved seeing her so engaged in the worship and prayer times and bringing memory verses home to learn. She would often come home after Kindy and lay her hands on my head and pray for me.

Each Wednesday night I held 'home church' with the girls in our lounge. We sang praise and worship songs, read from the Bible and prayed. I loved watching Ahnaliyah putting her all into the praise and worship. She would sing fervently, dance, and raise her hands in surrender to God. It was beautiful. The other two girls were a little older and not so keen to participate in house church, instead slouching in their seats giving me surly looks and asking if they could go to bed.

I soon found work as a 'Mystery Shopper', a fun and unique job where I visited stores and businesses posing as a regular customer, then went home and wrote up a report about the customer service I received and the cleanliness of the store. I signed up with over fifteen different mystery shopping companies. There were significant perks to this job—I received free petrol and groceries, free movie tickets, and more. I once got paid to test drive a brand new hundred-thousand-dollar BMW. For two years running I was a judge for the Hawke's Bay Wine Awards, visiting wineries around the region and doing wine tastings.

Mason and I were happy, enjoying each other's company and spending time as a family. But we were almost two years into our relationship and he had still not kissed me—and not for lack of trying on my part. I longed for that affection from him and wondered why he couldn't bring himself to kiss me? *What was wrong with me? Maybe if I was prettier,* I thought. *Maybe if I was browner. Maybe if I was skinnier. . .*

* * *

Shortly after we moved to Hastings, our family received the devastating news that my dad had been diagnosed with prostate cancer. It didn't seem real. It wasn't fair. But my dad, like our ancestors, was a man of great faith. My dad's battle with cancer was inspirational. He never complained and was a pillar of strength right to the end.

Dad made his last visit to Hawke's Bay in June 2010. After that, it became too uncomfortable for him to travel so far. He must have known it was going to be his last time in Hastings, because as he and Mum were heading out to the car to return home, he stopped, paused for a moment, turned around, looked me right in the eye and said, "I'm so proud of you Keren." I will never forget those words or the look in his eyes when he said them. It meant so much.

At eleven p.m. on a Sunday in October 2011, my dad went to be with Jesus. I was with him when he took his last breath and his spirit departed this earth.

I was heartbroken. That was my daddy, the daddy who camped out on the back of his truck or on the veranda at night to watch the stars and satellites with me, the daddy who took me out on the farm on his motorbike, the daddy who'd play his guitar and sing to me, the daddy who read from the Bible and prayed with me.

I was comforted in the knowledge that my dad, such a great man of God with an unwavering faith, was now beholding the glory of our Lord Jesus Christ. I cannot imagine the pure joy my dad experienced seeing Jesus face-to-face after spending his life loving, obeying, and believing without seeing. He was now able to see. He no longer had to guess, dream, and imagine what Heaven looked like because he was there.

* * *

Mason was beside me at Dad's funeral, and he was at my bedside when I was admitted to hospital for gall bladder surgery. He was at the girls' school prizegivings (all three girls were academic, often topping their classes and coming away with a hoard of awards each term), productions, kapa haka performances, and their sports games. He was at Ahnaliyah's bedside when she was rushed to hospital for an appendectomy. Although he never lived with us, he was the closest thing they had to a father-figure after Dad died. Likewise, I was there for his niece's and nephew's school galas, kapa haka performances, school productions, prizegivings, and cross-country races. I loved our big, blended family.

Mason, the girls, and I enjoyed many wonderful family holidays around New Zealand. We had several holidays in Auckland to visit friends and attend concerts. We also enjoyed time together and made lifelong memories in Taupo and Turangi.

Life with Mason was full and busy, but years into our relationship he had still not given me that romantic kiss I longed for. It seems ridiculous now that I kept waiting and hoping the affection and romance would magically kick in. It never did. I would make Mason give me a hug and kiss before he left my house after a visit but after a few seconds of hugging, he would push me away and say, "Okay, that's enough now," and the goodbye kiss was a quick peck, the same way he kissed his mother. We had some family photos taken. The photographer asked us to kiss, and the resulting photo shows Mason's reluctance and discomfort. It was so obvious that the photographer immediately apologised, asking if she'd misread our family dynamics and if we were actually a couple.

The proposal I hoped for never came either. Each birthday, Christmas, anniversary, and Valentine's Day I got my hopes up thinking this might be the day he finally got down on one knee and asked me to marry him. Mason kept making promises and giving timelines, but the dates would come and go with new reasons not to get married. First, he said I needed to move to Hastings so we could get to know each other, so I did. Then he said we had to wait until his niece started college.

After that, he said God told him we had to be together for seven years before we could marry. Seven years passed, and then Mason said we had to wait for his mum's retirement. I allowed myself to be led on for so many years.

I spoke to Mason about my desire to have a baby with him once we were married. I longed to share the magic of pregnancy, childbirth, and baby milestones with a father who was going to stick around and be a dad. I longed for that 'completed' family. Mason's response was confusing. "It doesn't make me less of a man if we don't have a baby, and it doesn't make you less of a woman," he said.

I wanted my girls to call him Dad, but he refused to let them do so. He also didn't want his niece to call me Aunty, despite the fact that I was her uncle's long-term girlfriend, and that he had her call virtually every other female in his life, 'aunty', even mere acquaintances. This lack of acknowledgement as family hurt me deeply. It really felt as though he wanted to keep me at arm's length, not wanting to fully let me in.

Mason and I once had an argument over the phone about the amount of time he spent with one of his friends, even sleeping at her house when refusing to sleep at mine. I didn't understand why she'd invite him to dinner and movie nights alone instead of inviting us as a couple. Having been hurt so many times in the past, I was still very insecure.

Soon I began spiralling and found myself having suicidal thoughts. I texted friends in Auckland who told me I had to get myself to hospital. I have no recollection of driving there that night, but I managed to get myself to the Emergency Department and my friend Lavina rushed to my side. When I called Mason, he refused to leave his friend's house to be with me in the hospital. He scolded me and said I would lose my girls because I had gone to the hospital and admitted to suicidal thoughts. His reaction shocked my friend. She said if it had been her in hospital, her husband would have moved heaven and earth to get there in an instant because, "That's what you do when you love someone."

After this incident I was diagnosed with depression and prescribed anti-depressants. In hindsight I suspect I'd suffered with mental illness for years due to the trauma of my past, but it had never been diagnosed. I started attending counselling. After many sessions, my counsellor suggested bringing Mason in to join us. He refused, saying I was the one who had issues and needed help, not him. Although he had seen me struggle with depression over the years, Mason was absolutely clueless about how debilitating mental illness can be. He constantly told me to just "wake up each morning and decide to be happy!" If only it were that simple.

I remember many a night spent crying alone on the floor of my ensuite, blasting worship music and crying out to God. I felt so alone, but the Holy Spirit was my comfort, and He met me on the bathroom floor. I often felt the warmth of His tangible presence envelop me in His love as the tears flowed.

* * *

When Janaya started acting out at around the age of nine, I blamed myself. Was it because of the abuse she had suffered and witnessed at the hands of her father? Was it because I had failed as a mother to give her the wonderful start in life she deserved? Was it because of all the moving from house to house during her formative years? Was it because I'd moved her away from her grandma and grandad who raised her? Was it because the grandad she loved so much had passed away?

She was getting in trouble at school, and at home we had to lock things away as she was stealing from her sisters and me. The constant lying and anger were emotionally exhausting. It really felt as if she hated me, and that broke my heart because I loved her beyond what any earthly words could describe. Her troublesome behaviour was causing me great concern, and I was reaching the end of my rope with her. I desperately wanted to know what was troubling her so I could help. I organised counselling, but the counsellor said Janaya refused to talk to her and that she just sat in the hour-long meeting looking at the floor and crying. What was going on with her? Why was she hurting so much? What could I do to take away her pain?

The school rang me one day to tell me about something she had done. I was on the verge of tears and needed to talk to Mason, to hear his voice. I called his phone and got no answer. He always caught a ride home with a workmate, so I sent her a text asking if he was with her in the hope that I could reach him on her phone. Mason was livid. He brought this incident up for years afterwards, especially during arguments, twisting it around and claiming I was 'checking up on him'. He even went to a counsellor about the incident, telling them I had been 'controlling'. This accusation hurt me deeply. I would never do to anyone what Dion did to me.

As the years went on, Janaya's behaviour grew worse. When she was around fourteen, she began sneaking out in the middle of the night, meeting up with complete strangers she had connected with online. I feared greatly for her safety. Who knew who these boys or men were? Who knew what they might do to her? I lost many hours of sleep trying to stay awake to hear her climbing out her window so I could stop her. After a week or so of this, the lack of sleep, stress, and utter exhaustion was taking its toll on me and even causing me to hallucinate. I didn't know what to do.

With Mason living out of town, I was raising these girls on my own and I struggled to cope. I'd phoned the police, child services, and several agencies to enquire what help was available, but no-one was willing to help. It was as if something terrible had to happen to my daughter before anyone would step up—an 'ambulance at the bottom of the hill' scenario. Desperately needing sleep, the only thing I could think to do was to put Janaya on a bus and send her to stay with my mum in Marton. This made Janaya even angrier and more hateful toward me, but I didn't know how else to protect her. I felt utterly inadequate as a mother.

She had a few weeks away at her grandma's, then came back home. At the age of fifteen, she ran away from home to move in with her boyfriend. Only then could I fully comprehend the pain Mum and Dad had experienced when I did the same thing. I got the police to bring her home several times, but she kept running back to him, and eventually the police told me not to phone them again.

It was the hardest thing in the world to let her go. She was still, and always would be, my baby 'Nah-Nah'.

I continued to worry about Janaya's safety, especially when the police turned up on my doorstep one day to tell me that a member of the public had phoned them about a physical altercation she and her boyfriend had had in the middle of town. My heart dropped in my chest with the realisation that history might be repeating itself in the life of my precious daughter. I felt so helpless. I wanted to protect my daughter from any kind of harm or heartache, and I felt that once again I'd failed her.

All I could do was pray for her and make sure I always had an open door for her to come home if she ever wanted to. I longed for the day that our relationship would be healed. I hoped that one day we would be able to enjoy each other's company and laugh together. I hoped one day we'd go out for coffee together and rebuild our mother-daughter relationship.

* * *

The three girls were growing up fast. In 2014 Janaya turned sixteen, Sanjanah was fourteen, and Ahnaliyah was ten. Janaya and Sanjanah hadn't seen their father since they were very small. We had protection orders out against him, but as teenagers they grew curious. They knew what he had done to us—I never hid that from them—but he was still their father, and they wanted to know more about him and where they came from. I knew the day would come eventually, and I knew I couldn't stop them from seeing him. I also knew he was a dangerous and violent man, so it had to be done safely.

It was arranged that Mason and I would take the girls to Marton to meet Dion. This was terrifying for me. For a long time after I left Dion, I had flashbacks of the abuse. Sometimes I was asleep and having a nightmare, but it also happened when I was wide awake. I might be alone at home, or in a room full of people—suddenly my mind would be transported back to a moment of violence I'd endured at his hands. It was like I was there and it was happening all over again.

These flashbacks while I was awake ceased after I gave my heart to Jesus, but I still had nightmares, and Dion's threats still wreaked havoc on my mind. I still feared he would come to kill me as he had promised he'd do if I ever left him. He had told me it could be years down the track, so I was living in constant fear. Each night I triple-checked that all the doors and windows of my house were locked. On stormy nights, I would lie in bed petrified. Amidst the howling wind and battering rain I would imagine I heard him breaking into the house to come and get me.

I had many sleepless nights leading up to our visit to Marton. All sorts of scenarios were running through my head. What if he had a weapon and attacked Mason? What if he grabbed the girls and ran off with them, or used this opportunity to fulfil his promise of killing me for leaving him? It was really hard for me, but I knew it was the right thing to do. I was so grateful that Mason insisted on going along with us.

The big day came far too quickly, and I felt sick during the entire drive from Hastings to Marton. My legs were shaking beneath me, threatening to give way, as we walked up to Dion's parents' house. I was on high alert in case I needed to intervene if he tried to hurt Mason or take the girls.

I needn't have worried. Dion was more nervous than I was. Sweat was pouring down his face, and he was trembling uncontrollably. In the end, I was so glad we went. I was no longer afraid of him after seeing him like this, and the girls' curiosity was satisfied. They had no desire to spend any more time with him. From that day onwards I have slept through stormy nights with absolutely no fear of him coming after me.

* * *

I enjoy spoiling the people I love on their birthdays. I like to give extravagant gifts, and over the years Mason and I were together, I celebrated his birthday with gifts, weekends away, and romantic, homemade dinners.

On Mason's forty-second birthday, the girls and I set up a treasure hunt for him, with clues hidden around the house. There were many clues to find, and these led to even more. Mason was beginning to tire of it all, until finally one clue led him to his present. He nervously unwrapped his gift and found tickets for a trip for two to the Gold Coast—flights, accommodation, and theme park admission included.

Three months later, we set off on our journey to the white sandy beaches of the Gold Coast. This holiday was a big deal for both of us. Mason had not been overseas before, and it was my first time leaving New Zealand in over twenty years. I also had high hopes that this trip would provide the perfect circumstances and setting for a marriage proposal.

Our apartment was on the seventh floor of the Surf Parade Resort. The view of the city lights from our balcony on the night we arrived was amazing, but the view of the crimson sunrise at four a.m. the following morning was even more breath-taking. We packed in as many activities as we could during our stay. Our trip was made even more special when we won accommodation at a resort in Bali.

The memories we made together on the Gold Coast were magical, and I knew I'd treasure them forever. We had dozens of photos, videos, and souvenirs to immortalise our time away. However, there was no affection or proposal in Australia, and I was disappointed yet again.

* * *

Life continued as usual when we arrived back in New Zealand. Mason and I argued about the lack of affection and commitment, and he often accused me of wanting everything my own way in the relationship. He'd say, "We're just not an affectionate couple," or "You're being impatient. You need to just enjoy the journey." I was frustrated and disheartened. He refused to kiss me. He even told me on numerous occasions that he found it irritating when I so much as touched him, going as far as to say it made his skin crawl.

One night, we stayed in a Palmerston North motel while visiting his brother who was unwell. Mason had a knack of falling asleep within minutes, while I took hours to get to sleep. This night, he fell asleep on his back. I took the opportunity to snuggle into him, resting my head on his shoulder. I was just starting to relax and drift off to sleep when Mason stirred. He realised I was cuddled close, and instead of rolling me gently away, he shoved me so hard that I flew off the side of the bed and onto the floor. My first instinct was to laugh, knowing he hadn't meant to push me that hard—he'd just woken and got a fright. He was terribly apologetic, which made it even funnier. I climbed back into bed and pulled the covers up only to find that Mason had built a pillow wall between us. He rolled over so his back was facing me. That's when it hit me and the tears began to flow. I cried myself to sleep realising that my own boyfriend didn't want me touching him. I longed for that physical touch, to feel wanted and loved. All I got from him was rejection and coldness. The relationship was abnormal, and the longer it went on, the more discontented, dejected, and resentful I became.

My frustration intensified as the years went by, and I became increasingly agitated by little things Mason did. I started to see him as old, doddery, and out of touch. The laugh I once found endearing now grated on my nerves. Despite all this, I loved him, and continued to hope things would change.

My family all loved Mason, but they were getting worried about me. My sister made several phone calls over the year following our Gold Coast holiday. We talked on the phone for hours. She encouraged me to leave because it had been almost eight years, and things were unlikely to ever change. She said she realised that Mason and I had a really amazing friendship and that he was such a good guy, but she also knew I wanted so much more. She knew I wanted love, affection, romance, and marriage. I knew she was right, but I wasn't ready to hear it. Mason and I had an incredible bond and so many years full of memories together. I loved him, but by this stage I was no longer 'in love' with him. All the years of him rejecting my affection had taken its toll on my romantic feelings for him, and although I hoped things would spark between us, I'd hardened my heart towards him.

* * *

In July 2015, Mason and I flew from Auckland to Bali via Sydney for another magical overseas adventure. I prayed that this holiday would be a turning point for us. I hoped Mason was planning a surprise proposal, and that a romantic spark would finally ignite between us.

We stayed at the stunning Ramada Resort in Nusa Dua. One of the highlights of our holiday was a visit to the Bali Safari and Marine Park. We chose the V.I.P. package and received the royal treatment. An elephant ride was part of the package. I'd looked forward to it the whole day but as soon as I got on, I was terrified. We were so high up, and I felt like I would fall forward over the elephant's head. The guide found it funny that I was so scared and he asked, "Are you scared ma'am? Don't be scared, miss. Just relax and enjoy it. It's a nice massage for your bum. It will get you all ready for later tonight." That made me laugh. If only he knew how unlikely it was that anything would happen that night or any night.

Indonesian currency had us feeling like millionaires. A hundred thousand rupiah was equal to about eleven or twelve New Zealand dollars. It felt strange to have millions of 'dollars'. Meals out cost us between 350,000-450,000 rupiah.

Mason and I enjoyed exploring the sights and sounds of Bali, but we were like two friends travelling together, not a couple in a romantic relationship. There was no affection and no proposal. I felt so rejected by his lack of interest in me as a girlfriend.

A sadness came over me as we packed our bags on our last morning in Bali; a realisation that we would never be more than friends. I felt empty and despondent on the journey home. I was furious, watching Mason strut along metres ahead of me in the airport, paying no attention as I struggled to carry my bags. I'd had enough of the apathetic relationship in which I felt unwanted and unloved. I was broken and lost.

I broke up with Mason several days after we arrived back in New Zealand. Our relationship had always lacked affection and intimacy, yet I was overwhelmed by a torrent of emotions—sorrow over losing my best friend of almost eight years, grief for the dreams I had for our future, regret for allowing myself to be led on for so many years, anger because he led me on and gave no affection, resentment for wasting so many years with Mason when I could have been with someone who wanted me (and for the possibility that my dad may have still been alive to walk me down the aisle), uncertainty for the future, and loneliness as I had moved away from my family for this man and now I was all alone.

I cried a little over the breakup, more like tears of disappointment over what could've been and the loss of the hopes and dreams I'd had for our future.

I had felt so rejected for so long that my romantic feelings towards Mason had waned before the breakup happened. I held on to the hope that romance, affection and commitment would magically materialise and our relationship would be saved. But over the years I realised that was never going to happen, and I had been questioning the longevity of our relationship for a long time.

Friends and family shook their heads in disbelief as years went by and I waited so patiently for him to marry me. "How much longer are you going to wait for him?" they asked, thinking I was a fool to believe things could ever be any different between us. I'd hoped and prayed things would miraculously change in Bali, but they didn't. Upon reflection, I think Mason loved me as a friend. He was never 'in love' with me, and the romantic feelings I had for him were never reciprocated.

I look back and wonder why I was so blind, why I ever thought our relationship would change. However, I will always be grateful to Mason and treasure the memories of our holidays overseas and in New Zealand and the fun times we had as a family. He opened my eyes and showed me a big wide world outside of my small country hometown of Marton.

8

Heartbreak and Miracles

By now, I was in my mid-thirties. I had packed up our lives and moved two hundred kilometres away from all our family and friends and everything we knew, and for what? I felt like I'd wasted so many years of my life on a relationship that was never destined to go anywhere.

Mason and I were over. I'd been with him for close to a quarter of my life. I didn't know what to do next.

I thought about moving back to Marton. But I remembered Manny Downs' prophecy from seven years earlier: "There are going to be times when you're over in Hastings that you're going to wonder if you made the right decision in moving. But God would have you know that He has planned this move for you, and it has been planned since before you were born. He has gone before you and made a way for you."

After much contemplation and prayer, I decided to stick it out in Hastings. The girls had friends. Sanjanah and Ahnaliyah were doing well in school and thriving in their church lives. I couldn't bear the thought of uprooting them again. Janaya was living with her boyfriend, and I didn't want to desert her by moving away.

I'd had almost twelve years with little or no affection. That situation was about to change in an unexpected and dramatic way when Joachim came into my life again and swept me off my feet.

Joachim began messaging me on Facebook shortly after my breakup with Mason. His messages were sweet and caring, and soon became charming and romantic, words of love I had been longing to hear. His messages and texts left me smiling from ear to ear. No one had ever spoken to me in this way before, and I felt loved. He expressed his feelings in a gentle, true, sensitive, and beautiful way. I learned that all those years ago when he had turned up at our church barbeque in Marton, he had not been there to see Kaz, but he had been there for me.

Joachim now worked as a sports coordinator and referee for a touch rugby company in Wellington. He had an inspirational work ethic, working long hours and putting a hundred percent into the job he loved. He had a company car and travelled extensively throughout New Zealand, and had the occasional international trip away. Affectionately known as 'Jo the Ref', he was admired and respected by his colleagues and friends. I also knew he had two daughters.

Joachim travelled to Hastings to see me on Christmas Eve 2015. I was as nervous as I had been before meeting Mason. Our messages, phone calls and texts had been flirty and romantic for months and yet I believed he would turn up, take a look at me and be so disappointed he would regret pursuing me and run in the opposite direction.

We planned for an overnight stay. Joachim would stay in the sleep-out as we were both Christians and wanted to 'do things right'. He would return to Wellington the next morning to spend Christmas Day with his family and I would head to Marton for a few days to have Christmas with mine.

Sanjanah was at Mum's place for the holidays, and Ahnaliyah was at a cookie decorating workshop that afternoon.

I was so nervous when I saw his car pull into the driveway. As I opened the front door to let him in, I was taken aback by his handsome looks. I felt myself blushing and stumbled over my words. We made our way to the kitchen, and I offered him coffee. "How many sugars do you take?" I asked, but I forgot to listen to his answer. I hesitated for a moment, embarrassed to ask again. "Sorry, how many sugars was that?"

I continued to stumble over my words, still too self-conscious to comprehend what he said. I was shaking so much the sugar was falling off the teaspoon until I didn't know how much I had put in his cup. He didn't say anything, so either it was right, or he was too polite to say and drank it regardless.

We sat on the back veranda, chatting as we drank our coffee. I was so shy. I felt like he was way out of my league and was probably wondering why he had bothered spending months pursuing me and why he'd driven all this way. All sorts of thoughts were running through my head, mostly negative. Surely he couldn't possibly be interested in someone who looked like me! We picked Ahnaliyah up from her workshop, then took a drive up Te Mata Peak.

The rest of that day is a blur. It all felt surreal, but when I woke up on Christmas morning, I smiled as I remembered my visitor outside. Was he awake yet? I worried about him seeing me without make-up first thing in the morning. We had breakfast together and I gave him his Christmas present, a twelve-dollar Taylor Swift calendar, a cheeky gift for a big fan!

The time for Joachim's departure was fast approaching. I didn't want him to go and had no idea when or if I would see him again. I needn't have worried. Joachim didn't want our time together to be over either. He asked if he could join me and my family for Christmas Day.

Joachim drove behind Ahnaliyah and I all the way to Marton,

where he met Mum, Janaya and her boyfriend and Sanjanah (who were already there for the holidays), my sisters, brother-in-law, and nephews. We initiated Joachim into the family with the mandatory ride on our 'world-famous-in-Marton' quadracycle. We shot box targets with my old bow and arrows and had water fights with the teenagers. I took him for a drive to the family farm where I was raised and told him about 'Heaven', my most cherished spot on the farm where Dad and I had our picnics.

Janaya pulled me aside at one stage and said, "He's cool, Mum. You should go out with him." Later that day, Sanjanah said the same thing. Everyone took an immediate liking to Joachim.

He left that afternoon to spend Christmas evening with his family and I lay in bed that night thinking about our time together. I was floating on air and hoped he felt the same. I didn't know when I would see him again. We had shared just two days together, and I wasn't sure how he felt about me.

I woke up on Boxing Day morning thinking of Joachim and smiled. Shortly after breakfast, he texted to say he was on his way back to Marton. I thought he was kidding because it was a long trip up from Wellington, but sure enough, he showed up. I felt so special that he'd travelled all that way to see me. I calculated that over that Christmas period, he drove nearly a thousand kilometres, and was on the road for around thirteen hours, all for me.

We spent Boxing Day playing Scrabble and being with my family. We rode up town with the kids on the quadracycle and bought takeaways for tea. Over dinner we discussed the End Times, and everyone joined in the conversation, even Mum and the girls. It was a perfect day. Joachim left again that evening. That night he sent me a text message that made me feel incredibly special.

I read the text over and over, trying to convince myself that this man really had these strong, genuine feelings for me. His words were intoxicating. I woke up the next morning to colours that looked brighter, air that felt fresher, and a world alive with promise.

* * *

Joachim came to visit me again in Hastings five days later so we could see in the New Year together. He drove via Marton so he could have a coffee and catch up with my mum and pick up Sanjanah after school holidays at her grandma's. Add another six hundred or so kilometres to the thousand he did over Christmas, and even after all that driving he insisted on cooking dinner for us when he arrived because I'd been working all day.

It had been a rollercoaster of a year. I thought about the trip to Bali with Mason and the breakup that left me feeling lost and alone, at my lowest point, but the year was ending on an unexpected, sudden and exciting high. Joachim had made me smile again. I couldn't wait to see what 2016 had in store for us.

We headed to the Sound Shell Amphitheatre on the Napier beachfront for the annual New Year's Eve celebrations. The place was packed, and instinctively I reached out to take Joachim's hand as we walked through the crowds to the venue. There was no forethought, but it felt right.

We sat on the grass, enjoying the concert. Joachim had his arms around me, and as midnight drew closer, I wondered if we would kiss when the clock ticked over to the New Year. I hadn't been kissed for twelve years. Would I even remember how? I wanted Joachim to kiss me. I was so accustomed to rejection I didn't know what to expect.

It was 11.59 p.m. when he pulled me close and kissed me, perfect and gentle. "You kissed me early!" I said. "I could tell you were nervous," he replied. "I wanted you to relax and enjoy the moment." He had read my mind.

The fireworks went off with thunderous bangs that vibrated in my belly and made me jump. Thousands of coloured embers filled the night sky, and Joachim hugged me from behind as we stood watching the dazzling display. I loved the feeling of his arms wrapped tight around my waist. He felt strong, and I felt safe, content, and tranquil. I didn't want the moment to end. I wanted to stay in the warmth of his embrace forever.

Joachim spent several days in Hastings and every moment was magic. We made trips to Maraetotara Falls and Waimarama Beach, and drank wine by candlelight while listening to music outside on the back porch as a thunderstorm raged around us. We cuddled on the couch and watched movies. We played mini golf. We had ice creams on the beach in Ahuriri. We fed the eels in the Clive Square fountain.

Joachim returned to Wellington after five days. He told me he felt like the luckiest guy, and assured me he'd return to me shortly. He referred to me as his 'relentless soulmate'.

Joachim dedicated the song *Back at One* by Brian McKnight to me. He said that the lyrics were 'our story in song'. The words were so special. *Crazy Love* by Brian McKnight, and *Weak* by SWV were also songs that meant a lot to us. One night while drinking on the veranda, I had played *Weak*. We had both consumed a substantial amount of alcohol, and as he listened to the words of the song Joachim began to cry, then came over and hugged me, saying how much he loved me and how he'd never felt that way about anyone else before. These three songs became 'our songs'. I listened to them all on repeat every night before I fell asleep.

Joachim visited often. I loved how it felt to melt into his arms. He held me so closely and tightly that I could feel his heart beating against my chest. Our bodies moulded together, and in that moment, we were one. I loved the way he gave me tender forehead kisses or kissed me with a passion that froze time. We were the only two people in the world.

He held my hand as we walked in public, kissing and hugging me in plain view, for all to see. Joachim was not ashamed to be with me. I loved the way he rested his hand on my thigh as we drove in the car, how he looked at me while saying how beautiful I was. I'd get shy and look away, but for the first time in my life, I began to believe it was true. He massaged my neck, shoulders and feet without being asked. He sat on the edge of my bed and played his guitar and sang to me.

Your entire perspective on life changes when someone loves and cherishes you in a way you've never experienced before. Joachim gave me everything I had ever wanted and needed. His love overwhelmed me because I had never felt anything like it before. I felt like the most special woman in the whole world. He broke down all the walls I'd built around myself. I trusted him and gave him my whole heart. Joachim was the man I had dreamed of since childhood.

* * *

The distance between us was hard to deal with. I sent Joachim a small gift in the mail each week so he would know I was thinking of him. He was busy at work, but made sure to phone several times a day to chat and see how my day was going. We spoke about him moving to Hastings and finding work. We discussed marriage and spending our lives together. I was the happiest I had ever been. Joachim was the man I would spend the rest of my life with. I thought I'd loved before, but nothing even came close to how I loved this man. We couldn't pass by each other in the house without hugging and kissing. I got butterflies when he came into the room. The chemistry between us was electrifying. We entered into a sexual relationship before marriage, despite my desire to do things God's way, and while it was wrong, it felt so right.

I had chosen Mason all those years ago, suffering through eight years of rejection when I could have been blissfully happy with Joachim all that time! I wondered where we would be now if I hadn't wasted my time with Mason. I wanted to turn back the clock so Dad could walk me down the aisle towards Joachim on our wedding day. I wished Joachim had known my dad so he could have seen what a great man he was.

I travelled to Paraparaumu at the end of January. Joachim was refereeing at a touch tournament and I sat on the side-lines, watching him in his element as he sprinted up and down the field. The young kids he was training looked up to him and thought the world of him. I fell more and more in love by the second.

Afterwards we went to the beach and lay together in the sand, enjoying the scenery while trying to figure out where to sleep that night. Neither of us had much money in our bank accounts, and after several hours of snuggling and dozing on the beach we ended up staying in a cabin at a campground in Levin. I was head over heels in love. Everything was perfect. Life was finally becoming what I'd always dreamed it'd be.

And then . . . he vanished!

He was gone from my life as quickly as he had appeared.

Joachim sent me a text saying that the long distant thing 'just couldn't work'. He couldn't leave his job. He had worked hard to reach a high level in his profession and had dreams and aspirations to go further.

* * *

A heavy darkness replaced the vibrant colour that had surrounded me throughout our whirlwind romance. I had believed with all my heart Joachim and I were 'the real thing' and would always be together. My heart shattered into a million pieces and I fell into severe depression. I was bedridden and suicidal. I had to take time off work. I turned to my default setting and began drinking heavily. I was pretty much always either sleeping, or crying and drinking. My poor daughters were basically left to fend for themselves. I was no good to anyone.

My pastor's wife, Rangiora, called in every day to check I was still alive. My doctors put me on a double dose of anti-depressants and had me see a psychiatrist. I started having serious panic attacks, so was prescribed a double dose of anti-anxiety meds. I spent my days crying in bed. After the girls had gone to sleep, I'd get up, sit outside in the darkness with headphones on, and blast music into my head at full volume. Tears streamed down my face, and I fell deeper and deeper into a dark abyss of depression.

I longed for Joachim to come back. My entire world was consumed by thoughts of him, memories of times we had together, what we did, things he had told me and promised me. I was positive the love we'd had was real, and I was sure he would eventually realise that and come back home to me. Every day I looked for him on my doorstep. If I did go out, I'd hurry home expecting to see his car parked in front of our house. My anticipation grew as I drove closer to home and I'd lean forward over the steering wheel as I turned into our driveway, hoping to find him there. He never was. Dejected beyond measure, I felt like I was drowning in an ocean of pain. It hurt to breathe.

Many people came alongside me during this time, visiting, bringing food, praying with me and prophesying over me. I attended church conferences, healing meetings, and prophetic meetings. I felt so lost and broken, and craved to soak in the atmosphere and presence of God. I always went along praying for a word of knowledge, some sort of encouragement, direction, or message of hope from God. I remember at one meeting the preacher was preaching and prophesying. I kept repeating over and over in my head this question to God, "Will Joachim come back? Will Joachim come back? Will Joachim come back?" Sometime into the meeting, amidst giving many prophecies, the pastor said, "I don't know who this is for, but God is telling you they will be back, and they will ask for forgiveness." I grabbed hold of that word and claimed it as my own.

Many of my friends and family thought I was foolish for holding out hope for Joachim, or even wanting him back after how much he had hurt me. The girls hated him for leaving the way he did. They saw the toll it took on me. It must've been an awful time for them when I was bedridden, constantly crying, and wanting to end my life.

As the weeks and months went on, I slowly started coming out of my hibernation and stopped the excessive drinking. I began walking up Te Mata Peak at least once every day. I put on my earphones and took my pain and frustration out on the asphalt as I slogged my way up the gradient of the hill. I actually looked forward to these daily walks amongst the trees. The nature and fresh air worked wonders on my mental health. I also lost a lot of weight and became the fittest I'd ever been. My sister Melissa, Sanjanah, Ahnaliyah, and I even conquered the eleven-kilometre Manawatu Gorge Track.

I still waited every day for Joachim to text me or call. He did text now and then over the months, telling me he missed me, how he thought of me often, and that I was the only girlfriend he'd ever had who treated him like a king. We made plans to meet up, but they always fell through at the last minute. There was less and less communication as the months went by. The words he texted grew colder and more distant. I pined for him. I wanted the love back that we'd had at the beginning of the year. He was on my mind every day, from the moment I woke until I closed my eyes at night.

I considered suicide several times that year but I didn't want to end my life. I wanted to end the pain and the hopelessness.

Driving to Marton with Ahnaliyah one day, I was thinking of Joachim. As the music blasted, I felt an all-encompassing sensation of numbness and darkness. There is a large tree at a fork on the windy road leading into Halcombe, and as I approached it, a powerful vortex pulled me towards it. The only thing I could see was the tree, standing out with clarity amidst a blurry haze. A magnetic force was pulling the car into the tree, and I struggled with the steering wheel to stay on the road. I remember thinking that if Ahnaliyah hadn't been in the car, I would've gone with the pull, driven straight into that tree, and ended it all. My life wasn't worth living, but Ahnaliyah had her life ahead of her with so much to live for. I am so glad she was with me that day.

Looking back, I realise that Satan, who loves to steal, kill and destroy, was trying to take me out and prevent me from fulfilling my purpose in life.

I started taking pottery classes to keep myself busy. I signed up to a Certificate in Money Management course, and took various spiritual growth courses. At one of them, God spoke profoundly clearly to me about my job. At the time, I was providing in-home childcare with a local agency. He encouraged me that my job was not simply a job, but an opportunity to represent Him and to practically minister to the families I served. He said:

"Love the families. Invite them to church events and don't be put off if your invites are rejected. You may be the only source of Jesus these children and their families have. Make a lasting impression on their lives and simply be yourself."

I was encouraged, and set up a 'ministry account' where each payday I could put some money aside. That way, whenever a need arose within the families whose children I cared for, I'd use that money to help them out, usually anonymously, sneaking grocery vouchers or money for clothing into their mailboxes without being seen. I also helped families with cough medicine, warm blankets, and more. It was a blessing to be able to bless others.

* * *

After a dark year, a beacon of hope and brightness came into our lives when we found out Janaya was pregnant. The prospect of a precious new baby in the family was the life-saving tether I needed to pull myself from the mire that surrounded me. At thirty-five, I felt too young to be a Grandma or Nanny, so I became 'Mema'.

I went with Janaya to her midwife and ultrasound appointments. Tears came to my eyes as I heard the beating of my grandbaby's heart, marvelled at the miracle of his perfect little body on the screen, and saw his mum's belly swell as he grew. There was great excitement in the household as the time drew closer for his grand entrance into the world. In preparation, we had a family photo shoot with Janaya and her boyfriend, George, Sanjanah, Ahnaliyah, and I. The photos captured the magic and joy of the upcoming addition to the family, and I couldn't wait to meet him.

My grandson, Cassius, was born on a Saturday in August. I was blessed to see him make his entry into this world. The moment I laid eyes on him he stole my heart. There are no words to describe the feeling of holding your baby's baby. I loved him beyond words, my little prince.

Cassius, Janaya, and George lived with me for several months after the birth. I saw Cassius every day and loved him so much that I ached when we were in different rooms. My troubles melted away when I held him in my arms. I loved every ounce of him. After Joachim left, I was broken. Now, this little boy saved my life.

* * *

Ten months later, Joachim came back.

He stayed with me for three nights while the girls were in Marton at Mum's place. I decided not to sleep with him. For a start, he was not my boyfriend anymore, let alone my husband, and I had no idea how many women he'd slept with over the past ten months. I had asked God's forgiveness for sleeping with him in the first place, breaking twelve years of 'born-again virginity', and was determined to wait for marriage. But, as they say, 'the best laid plans…'

I had pined for months, lost hope I would ever see him again, and there he was at my door. When we hugged, it felt like home. We slept together several times during his visit. Before he left, he looked me in the eye and asked if I was going to be okay. I burst into tears because I didn't want him to leave again. He hugged me tight and said he'd be back. I shook my head in disbelief. He assured me he would return, and soon.

I wanted those frequent, beautiful, and loving texts I used to get after a visit from Joachim. He did text me a couple of times, but the words were distant and cold, and my heart broke all over again. I wanted to return to the way we were earlier in the year. Where did that love go? Were we just 'friends with benefits' now? Was that all I meant to him?

I loved him—or perhaps I loved the memory of the person he was a year earlier. I deserved to be loved by someone who would prioritise me in their life and make me feel special and worthwhile.

I knew all this, but I didn't know how to let go of Joachim. I believed I was going to grow old with him. I was heartbroken, confused, and unable to cope. The pain went on and on. I did not know how to make it stop, to make things better, to stop the hurt, the pining, and the memories.

Joachim made several visits over the following months. I convinced myself he kept travelling all the way from Wellington because, deep down, he loved me. But after he left, I wouldn't hear from him again for weeks. After each visit I was broken all over again. The pain, confusion and darkness were debilitating.

In July 2017, Joachim asked me to join him at his daughter's kapa haka performance in Napier, saying it would 'mean so much to him' if I went. I hesitated because he'd been and left so many times. But who was I fooling? I still loved him and would've given anything to see him again.

I agreed to go, providing he refrain from hugging or even touching me because I was sick and tired of him getting what he wanted and leaving.

I picked him up from his Airbnb the evening before the kapa haka and we had coffee at McDonalds. I tried so hard to act nonchalantly, but inside I was melting in his presence. It felt so good to be with him again. I loved him so much it felt like a crime for us to ever be apart. We drove around the port and then parked up overlooking the water.

He calmed my anxiety by playing icebreaker-type games, and soon we were laughing like we did in the good days. Then our conversation took a more serious turn, and he apologised for leaving me, for not being there when I was battling depression and suicidal thoughts. He asked if I could ever forgive him for what he had put me through. It was the first time he acknowledged what he'd put me through by leaving the way he did. Later that night when I dropped him back at his accommodation I stuck to my guns when he tried to hug me goodnight. I told him it was just too hard knowing he would leave me again for however many months.

The next night he made me dinner. We decided to take a nap before heading to the kapa haka. Joachim offered me the bed and asked me if I wanted him to sleep on the couch. "You can sleep next to me," I said, "but we are just going to sleep." He lay down beside me and hugged me from behind. I closed my eyes, breathing in his familiar scent, feeling safe, content and tranquil, just as I'd felt on the night we watched the New Year's fireworks at the Sound Shell. The electricity between us was so strong. Sleep was impossible, and we made love. I kicked myself afterwards for letting that happen again.

We showered and headed to the Municipal Theatre for the kapa haka competition. Joachim was a very proud dad. He had his arm around me the entire night, and it felt so good. Afterwards, when we parked up at the beach, I didn't want our time together to end. We fell asleep together in the car.

I was holding back tears when I dropped him off at his accommodation shortly after midnight. The next day he was going to drive back to Wellington, and every part of me was sure he'd go cold on me again. He sensed I was about to cry and asked how I'd feel about him visiting more often. I thought it was just a line to make me feel better. "I'd like that," I said, "but I don't believe you mean it."

* * *

We got back together the following month. I had been telling people for more than a year it had been true love and that he'd be back. They didn't believe me and when it happened, I felt like shouting from the rooftops, "I told you so!"

This time he was all in. He left the job that meant so much to him and moved to Hastings. I'm a sucker for romantic movies and Joachim leaving and then returning to me translated as 'our happily ever after'. It was just like Johnny driving away leaving Baby in *Dirty Dancing,* only to return at the end and sweep her off her feet in a big dance routine, or when Edward returns to Vivian in *Pretty Woman,* waving roses from the sunroof of the limousine and facing his fear of heights to climb up the fire escape to her top-floor apartment. This was my happy ending. A love story ten years in the making.

The love, romance and affection were back. Life was blissfully beautiful again. I felt my eighteen months of waiting were justified because he was now in Hastings, having given up everything to be with me and begin our lives together.

Joachim had recommitted his life to Jesus and had been attending a course at his church. I noticed the transformation right away. He had given up drinking and some other vices he'd struggled with over the years. He prayed with me every night, holding my hands in his, before he went outside to the sleep-out. He did Bible studies and devotions every day and integrated himself into my church family and church life.

Joachim cleaned out my car shed and turned it into a man-shed where he set up his drumkit and a makeshift office. I loved hearing him out there playing the drums, and often spent a lot of time there, adoring him as he played. He also spent many hours in there looking and applying for work so he could help contribute to the running of the household.

He woke up at five o'clock every morning, and while I slept he cleaned the house for me before he headed to the gym. He helped me cook dinner, did the dishes, fixed my car, spent hours doing the gardening and maintenance around the house. He taught Ahnaliyah to play the drums, took Sanjanah for driving lessons, and helped me with my homebased childcare business. I felt blessed beyond words.

* * *

I have always loved photos. They capture precious moments for generations to come, and I had enjoyed several photo sessions to record the stages of my growing family. Joachim knew about this and suggested we have a couple shoot. I loved the idea, so we booked it with a photographer who had done several shoots for me over the past couple of years.

As much as I enjoy the photos when they're done, I'm always self-conscious at a shoot. Despite my awkwardness, I loved every moment having photos taken with the love of my life, capturing our reconciliation and the beginning of our 'growing old' together.

We were walking across a bridge during the shoot when Joachim stopped, grabbed me by the waist, looked into my eyes and told me how much he loved me and how happy and blessed he felt to be loved by me. Falling down onto one knee, he revealed a ring that he seemed to pull out of thin air. As soon as I realised what was happening my heart started racing. I could barely breathe. My legs turned to jelly. My head was spinning. I'd dreamed of this moment my whole life. All the pain and heartache had led me to this magical moment, and I felt like I was about to black out.

I don't remember what Joachim said but I do know he talked a lot. He was no stranger to public speaking and was involved with Toastmasters, so I'm sure whatever he said was perfect. I said yes. He stood up and slid the ring onto my finger. Life stood still for several moments as we hugged and kissed there on the bridge. The photographer was taking photos of us from many different angles, and she captured this beautiful, life-changing moment on camera for us to treasure forever. She hadn't known it was going to happen—she was as clueless as me. It was a magical day forever ingrained in my memory.

Joachim had been messaging Janaya, Sanjanah and Ahnaliyah about his plan for some time, and I now understood why they'd told me to paint my nails for the photo shoot. Mum had also known because he had been to Marton to ask her permission.

To say I was over the moon would be a huge understatement. It all felt like a dream I never, ever wanted to wake up from.

Wedding plans were soon underway, and Joachim took the driver's wheel. He kept a diary for our brainstorming and organising, everything from the date, venue and photographers, to our first dance, flowers and wedding party. He designed our invitations and wrote the names of our guests in beautiful calligraphy. He wrote detailed run sheets for the day. He knew exactly what needed to be done to make our big day perfect.

Our wedding was set for 28th January 2018, just over four months after our engagement. It was all go. I was blessed that in his will, Dad had left some money specified for my wedding day. We booked *The Old Church* in Taradale for an outdoor ceremony in the picturesque courtyard. This would be followed by a reception underneath the grand chandelier in the fairytale-like main hall. We booked the same photographer who had been at our engagement and had captured so many other special moments for our family.

I shopped for my wedding dress at The Bridal Studio in Palmerston North. Mum, Janaya, Ahnaliyah and baby Cassius joined me on this momentous day. It was so special to have them there. I felt so pampered and tried on several dresses, but when I tried on *the dress,* I knew it was the one—a gorgeous off-the-shoulder white dress with a short train. I couldn't wait for Joachim to see me in it as I walked towards him on our wedding day.

Janaya, Sanjanah and Ahnaliyah were to be our bridesmaids, and we bought them beautiful dresses. I didn't understand why Joachim didn't want his own daughters to be part of the bridal party. I thought it would have been lovely having all five of our girls standing with us. In any case, Cassius was the page boy, and Joachim asked Janaya and Sanjanah's boyfriends to be his groomsmen. My eldest sister, Melissa, agreed to walk me down the aisle in Dad's stead. My pastor, Peter Brothers, would marry us and Joachim's friend Rikki would sing our song *Back at One* as I walked up the aisle. Our first dance was going to be to Ed Sheeran's *Thinking Out Loud*.

We bought our rings and shoes, ordered the bouquets and flowers, and picked up our wedding license. We selected our canapés, entree, dinner and dessert menus. We booked the make-up artist, hairdressers and ordered the cake. We sent out invitations, and excitement escalated as our special day approached.

One morning, Joachim went out and returned home with a big smile on his face. He asked me to guess where he'd been. He had driven all over town visiting different motels, checking out the colours and lighting in the rooms to find the perfect place for the girls and I to spend the night before the wedding and to have photos taken as we got ready the next day. This sweet gesture brought tears to my eyes. I was living in a fairy tale.

And then everything turned dark.

Joachim started drinking again. He spent a lot of time lying in bed, which wasn't like him at all. When I tried to talk to him, he shut me out. The affection faded away. He barely spoke to me. I thought maybe he was feeling down because nothing had eventuated from his ceaseless job hunting despite a number of interviews. I thought maybe he felt bad for not contributing anything towards the bills, food, and wedding costs.

Seven weeks before the wedding, Joachim told me he would head down to Wellington to do a few weeks' work to get us some money for Christmas and our big day. I paid for him to get a haircut on the morning he left, and bought his bus ticket to Wellington.

He never came back.

* * *

When I realised what had happened, everything fell apart. He had promised to never hurt me or leave me again. I was devastated beyond belief, abandoned, alone, and destitute.

I was left to cancel the venue, the photographer, the cake-maker, the make-up artist, the hairdresser.

I returned the bridal party shoes and the wedding rings.

I contacted guests to say the wedding was off.

The cancellations were close to the day, so I lost money on most things. The pain, betrayal, and abandonment I felt was made worse by the guilt I felt over wasting Dad's money. I had used my own money too and lost much of it. Joachim hadn't spent a penny. My tears turned to bitterness, cynicism and hard-heartedness.

Darkness threatened to overcome me once again.

My saving graces were my faith in God, my beautiful daughters, and my adorable grandson. I would not have made it without these blessings. Because of them I had a reason to get up each day and carry on.

One day my darling grandson came running into the lounge, buck naked after his bath. He wanted to hand me something, so I took the bit of paper from his chubby little hand and screamed with delight when I realised it was an ultrasound photo. Cassius was going to be a big brother! I loved Cassius with all my heart, and now this new precious addition to our family would fill my heart even more.

My beautiful granddaughter, Evei-Manea was born on a Thursday in March. I was overjoyed to be in the delivery room and see her enter the world.

I felt overwhelming love and pride for Janaya and for the new baby. She was perfect. I couldn't get enough of her tiny little fingers and toes. The entire family came to visit shortly after Evei was born. As I watched Cassius kissing and cuddling his baby sister, it was almost too much sweetness for my heart to handle. Evei was lying on her mum's chest, and Cassius was sitting next to them both on the bed. As Cassius spoke, Evei turned her head to look at him as if she recognised his voice, and the tears welled in my eyes. It was a poignant moment of sibling bonding.

The arrival of this precious angel was a Godsend, bringing joy and light to dispel the darkness of my broken heart.

9

A Moment with God

When I saw my reflection in the bathroom mirror, I barely recognised the person looking back at me. I looked so tired, so worn down from the disappointments and heartaches that had besieged the past twenty years of my life. Tears streamed down my face and blurred my vision. I covered my mouth to muffle the sobs that came from somewhere deep inside as I continued to stare at my forlorn image in the mirror. I felt somewhat detached from myself. *Who was I? How did I get here? Why did life hurt so much? What happened to the dreams I'd had as a child?*

"Jesus, where are You?" I whispered between sobs. "Jesus, please help me . . . I need You . . . I can't do this on my own."

I was determined to avoid the overwhelming darkness I'd experienced after the first time Joachim left, so I took a short time off work to adjust to my new reality. I cried a lot, then quickly put on my big-girl pants, slapped on a smile, and threw myself into work. In order to avoid feeling anything, I went into complete autopilot mode, keeping myself busy from the moment I opened my eyes in the morning until I collapsed into bed each night.

Whenever I was around people, I forced a smile to mask what was really going on inside. Nobody knew the depth of my pain. In my mind I was screaming, "Please someone see me! Like, truly see me! Am I so insignificant that you can look straight through me? Am I that worthless that you can turn a blind eye? Please someone understand me! Please someone care! Please someone help me! I'm tired of being alone! I'm tired of feeling isolated! I'm tired of battling on my own! *I'm tired!*" But I just kept going, burying my suffering, and suppressing my broken heart.

Late at night, as I lay in bed all alone, the tears kept coming and the overthinking still haunted me. I thought back over the years of failed relationships and told myself that I was the common denominator in all of them and it must've been my fault that none of them lasted. I returned to my old thoughts: *If only I were more beautiful; if only I were skinnier; if only I had a perfect smile; if only I weren't so shy and awkward . . .*

At almost forty, I believed I was too old to ever find the love I'd dreamed of all my life. I felt I was past my use-by date. I'd always wanted to share my life with one man, but my life was already half over and I had missed my opportunity. The grief of those unfulfilled dreams and expectations was all-encompassing. In the words of Proverbs 13:12, unrelenting disappointment had left me heartsick.

I cried in the shower, I cried until my pillow was soaked, yet every morning I got up, put on a fake smile, and did what needed to be done.

I continued providing the homebased childcare I'd been doing for six years, added before and after school care, offered babysitting in people's homes in the evenings and weekends, and worked as a respite carer one weekend a month for a little boy with autism. I worked an average of seventy hours each week for almost two years. One week I racked up over ninety-eight hours.

I had no downtime. I often didn't have time or energy to even shower. I had children in my home from as early as six-thirty in the morning until around six o'clock in the evening. During winter I'd start work when it was still dark outside, and finish when it was dark again. But work didn't end once the children went home each night. After cooking dinner, I'd spend hours writing in the children's journals, cleaning, filling in a seemingly endless pile of forms and paperwork, and preparing play activities and arts and crafts for the following day. I was often still working at ten or eleven o'clock at night. I'd no sooner fall into bed then my alarm would go off and I'd have to do it all over again.

Everything felt like a chore. Going to the toilet, eating … it all just wasted precious time.

Sanjanah and Ahnaliyah were always asking me, "Why are you so angry, Mum?" The answer is, I was simply not coping. The exhaustion was overwhelming.

The busyness left little time for me to grieve Joachim and all the hopes and dreams I had for our lives together. I switched off from feeling, and lived on autopilot to survive. There was no time to slow down, relax or spend quality time with my family. There was no time to just breathe. It wasn't sustainable. I was a single mum running a household on my own, working way too much. It was no surprise when I was diagnosed with burnout in December 2019.

I took two weeks off work to rest up and then started back with 'reduced' hours that still totalled over forty per week. It didn't help the exhaustion. The damage had been done, and it would take more than just two weeks to fix it. I was exhausted—soul, heart, and bone-tired— yet I stuck it out at work.

When I first started work as a homebased carer in 2014, I felt like I had stumbled across the dream job. I had always adored babies, and the idea of getting paid to spend my days with these precious little ones seemed too good to be true. Back then I would stand at my window each morning eagerly waiting for the children to arrive so I could cuddle them and dote on them. There were even times I would naughtily wake them from their naps because I missed them and wanted to snuggle them. Back then my job seemed to be all about providing a safe haven for the babies while their parents were at work, studying, or having some time out—a place where the babies felt loved and secure, where they had fun and laughed, somewhere they looked forward to coming each day.

But as the years went on, the red tape from the Ministry of Education made the job less about the children and more about a ridiculous barrage of rules and regulations, paperwork and forms, procedures and policies. The bureaucracy stole all the joy and love from the job, and I became increasingly resentful towards the powers that be. It wore me down. Six years later, I no longer waited eagerly each morning for the children to arrive. Instead, I dreaded waking up each morning to face another day.

As the exhaustion took over, I became apathetic in my work. I remember struggling with the simplest tasks around the house. Even walking felt like an exercise in concentration. I had to focus on each and every step, lifting one foot off the ground and putting it back down in front of the other. My legs felt like they were weighed down with lead, too heavy to move. I sat in my car and talked myself through the steps of turning it on: "Put key in the ignition, foot on the brake, foot resting on the accelerator, turn the key, footbrake off, put the gear stick into drive, slowly take your foot off the brake and slowly push on the accelerator." My brain would shut down as I drove and I'd have no idea why I was in the car. I'd pull over to the side of the road to compose myself and think about what I was doing and where I was going. I often found I was heading in the wrong direction and had to turn around.

I was completely rundown, exhausted and overwhelmed. I knew I couldn't keep up with the demands of the job and the long hours.

My heart was heavy when I told my families I would be finishing up in April at the end of the term. It was so hard. I'd looked after many of these children since they were infants and loved them all dearly. Their families had become like family to me. To this day I feel bad for letting these families down after we'd developed such strong bonds.

* * *

At the beginning of March 2020, Ahnaliyah was fifteen years old and in hospital for surgery. While she was in theatre, I met up for coffee with a friend in the hospital cafeteria. Clearly, I wasn't doing well. He recalls:

"Life decided to throw a few bombs Keren's way, and she experienced high burnout. It was horrible to see. The long hours, the stress, the preparation, family issues, and that major heartbreak had taken its toll once again. With no time to think for herself, or even the energy to take a break and go out fishing or play mini-golf with me, or even to just have a coffee, this began to eat away at her. I began to see Keren wither away. One day I met with Keren at the hospital where her daughter was having surgery. It was the only time that could be spared to meet with a friend. I took it without any hesitation as I knew she needed to vent and be listened to. During this conversation I could see a huge burden on her shoulders, and a numbness over her. Things were taking a terrible toll on my friend emotionally, financially, and on her soul. I felt helpless as her friend. I wanted to do anything I could to take it all away, but I'm only human, and so I presented her to the Lord. I asked that He would minister to her and reach her heart in a way that only He could."

Towards the end of March, I finally fell apart and crumbled into a heap on my bed. I couldn't stop crying. I was jittery, shaky and couldn't concentrate. I couldn't go another day without losing my mind. Unable to carry on, I was forced to resign immediately, three weeks earlier than planned. The extreme exhaustion, lethargy and inability to function normally, were all symptoms of a nervous breakdown.

I felt as if I'd been fighting a war my entire life. I was soaked in pain and sadness for all my disappointments, the heartbreaks, the feeling that no matter how hard I tried things always ended up the same.

* * *

Around that time, the Covid-19 pandemic was spreading across the globe like wildfire. News reports told of thousands of people dying every day. In New Zealand, as in many countries, life came to a grinding halt as workplaces, schools, universities, churches, travel and borders were closed. Entire countries were put into lockdown. People were told not to leave their homes. Bustling metropolises became eerie ghost towns.

Some beautiful stories rose from around the world during this time. In Venice, with crowds diminished, the canals became crystal clear. Swans returned, and fish could be seen swimming about clearly. Even dolphins and an octopus were spotted meandering up the usually busy waterways. In Italy, people stood on their balconies playing instruments and singing together, united in their solidarity. Air pollution was dramatically reduced, and people in India reported they could see the Himalayas more than a hundred miles in the distance for the first time in decades.

In New Zealand, we had time to observe and prepare before the virus reached our shores. Our first case of Covid-19 was reported on the 28th of February 2020. Deciding to stop the spread of the virus in its tracks, the government implemented an early lockdown. Three days after I had crumbled onto my bed in a state of breakdown, the nation went into the highest level of lockdown. No one was allowed to leave their homes unless for essential reasons. It was a frightening and uncertain time as the world grappled with health and economic emergencies.

At the time, it seemed unreal, like a movie about a deadly virus outbreak. Just a week earlier we had been going about life as usual, and now the entire country had come to a standstill. Things happened so fast. The world changed in an instant.

I was immensely grateful for the time of enforced rest. I often joked that I prayed for some rest, and God responded by shutting the entire world down just for me! On the first day of lockdown, I wrote the following entry in my journal:

26th March 2020

I'm loving lockdown! I lay in bed this morning, the first morning of our nation's lockdown and everything was so beautifully serene, still and calm. No traffic noise, just birds singing. I spent today in the garden, and then, for the first time in years, I sat on the veranda listening to music and enjoying the sunshine. I've also packed up all my work equipment, so for the first time since we've lived in this house our home is just a home not a workplace. I'm so relieved to finally be able to just stop. I've been non-stop crazy busy for so many years. This is the first break I've had in a very long time. I'm already starting to feel slightly more human and it's only Day One.

Sanjanah had been studying at Bible College in Auckland and I was thrilled when she came home to isolate with us. She continued with her studies, as did Ahnaliyah with her schoolwork, via distance learning and online classes. It was such a strange time to be alive!

I had weeks to rest and recover from my breakdown. I really felt a huge weight lifted from my shoulders. I stopped, took time to breathe, and began to process some of the past trauma and heartbreak, and allowed myself to truly feel the pain of the wounds that had been festering in my heart for many years, rather than subduing it.

For many years, I'd battled daily with depression and anxiety, never getting time to pause, instead carrying on while dragging the weight of mental illness along for the ride. Being able to completely stop and to live purely in the moment was a very therapeutic opportunity for healing and self-discovery.

On the 13th of April, 2020, I had a profound encounter with God. It was eighteen days into our first lockdown, twenty-one days since I had finished working. Lying in bed that night, God said to me, "Open the curtains. Look at the night sky."

I pulled back the curtains, climbed back under the warmth of my blankets, and lay crossways on my bed so I had a front row seat to the midnight scenery. There was a half-moon, stunningly bright, and it illuminated the darkness. I could see the shadows on the moon's surface. I could see a handful of stars, and two were much brighter than the others.

I was entranced by the gentle way the clouds moved across the sky and everything darkened a little as they passed in front of the silver lunar light. The moon cast a halo glow as it shone through the clouds. The outer ring of the halo was tinged by a rusty, golden light. From time to time the cloud was so dense that the moon almost disappeared from view and when it passed, the renewed brightness of the moon was almost blinding as my eyes readjusted to the light.

I admired the wonders and beauty of the night sky and felt an inexplicable peace, unlike anything I'd experienced in many years. I was totally present, and for the first time in a very long time my mind was clear. I felt no concern for the things I hadn't done that day, and no worry over what I needed to do tomorrow. I looked at the time and was surprised to see an hour had passed. I focused again on the beauty framed by my bedroom window and thought about the sheer vastness of the universe and God's infinite creation. I remembered nights as a child on our family farm, sleeping outdoors, star-watching with my dad and spotting satellites and shooting stars.

After a while, the earth rotated and the moon disappeared above the house and out of view. I stared at a solitary wisp of cloud below the two brightest stars. The clouds were no longer moving in the sky; they were fixed in place at that moment. Several hours passed as I lay spellbound by the beauty of the cosmos but it seemed more like a matter of minutes. I closed my eyes several times but sleep eluded me. When I opened my eyes, I was greeted by an ever-changing panorama. A few wispy clouds became a full, thick fluffy blanket, and the clear skies began to drop rain.

The darkness began to dissipate as the new day dawned. Different layers, textures and shades of grey cloud looked like brush strokes in a beautiful painting. Trees became visible as dark silhouettes against the sky. Birds began to wake and fly with grace across the wide expanse. I watched in awe, admiring the intricate beauty as the grey clouds folded themselves away to reveal windows of blue sky. The trees shook off their dark shadows, and each became a palette of contrasting, vibrant greens.

I had been awake all night but felt no anxiety over the lack of sleep. The peace I felt was deep and profound, and I was not the least bit tired. The sun shone and a new day began. I felt content and refreshed after dwelling in God's presence all night.

A memory of my grandma came to mind. She always said, "The break of dawn is the best part of the day." I stayed with her often and I remembered hearing her moving about in the early hours of the morning while it was still dark outside. As soon as the sun peaked above the horizon she was usually out tinkering in her beloved garden. I now understood the beauty and tranquillity of the first light of day that she spoke of and loved so dearly.

This night of basking in the glory of God's creation was a significant encounter of His love. There was no physical manifestation, no audible voice from Heaven, no supernatural signs or wonders, no visions or angelic visitations. It was a precious time of encountering His love and peace; intimate, gentle, and calming.

God spoke to me about several things during this time of stillness and serenity. He told me to start writing again. He specifically told me He wanted me to write my life story. He kept emphasising the importance of this throughout the night.

He also expressed His desire to see me begin to enjoy my life rather than merely enduring it, and He gave me guidance towards living the abundant life He intended for me. He gave me some practical instructions to improve my emotional wellbeing, ways to simplify my days, focus on what is really important, and live in the moment.

I talked to Him about the fact that I was turning forty in six months and that I was still unmarried and feeling disappointed, rejected, and sorrowful. Life had not panned out the way I'd dreamed and imagined it would. I confided in Him, unburdened myself. As I did so, I no longer felt overwhelmed by the heartache and regret that usually accompanied these thoughts. I was comforted and reassured. He knew me better than I knew myself. He understood the desires of my heart more intimately than I did. I truly felt I had been given the chance to start over and to live the life God intended for me. I knew my story was not over.

Epilogue

I've known about Jesus all my life. When I was a little girl, Jesus was part of my family's everyday conversation. My parents lived and breathed Christianity. We went to church every Sunday, attended home groups every Wednesday night, prayed together, read and discussed the Bible, and regularly socialised with other Christian families. In my childlike faith, I never questioned His existence. He loved me and lived inside of me, and that was that.

Even when I strayed and was living a life contrary to what I knew was right, I still believed in Him. The topic of God occasionally popped up in the midst of drunken parties, and I'd bring my Bible out to try and convince people that He was real. My skinhead friends mocked and pretended that the Bible burned their eyes when they looked at it and scorched their fingertips if they touched it.

When I came back to Jesus at the age of twenty-three, I discovered a love for studying the Bible. I also became interested in looking deeper into why I believed what I believed. I was fascinated to discover that there is an abundance of evidence for Jesus outside of the Bible. I pondered the thought that if I had known about the extensive historical information and evidence for Jesus and His crucifixion, would I have made different choices in my life?

However, for many years I had only ever had 'head' knowledge, not 'heart' knowledge. I knew all the Bible stories and scriptures. I knew the theology and principles of Christianity, I believed God could speak to us (I'd heard His voice myself), and I knew He was a God of miracles

(I'd seen miraculous healings right in front of my eyes). But despite all this, it wasn't until many years later, when I was thirty-nine years old and spent a moonlit night in God's presence that I felt that 'head' knowledge finally permeate my heart and change my entire perspective on life as I encountered God's love for me.

I had allowed the Enemy to overwhelm me for years with feelings of guilt and condemnation for all the wrongs I'd done in my life, especially those transgressions I'd committed after I had been born again. I felt I had failed in my walk with God. I knew, in my head, that He still loved me and that He had forgiven me, but I felt unworthy of His love and grace because I had knowingly and willingly sinned.

Fortunately, God is not a 'three strikes and you're out' God. He does not condemn us. Satan does that. God's grace is sufficient, and His mercies are new every morning. This is no 'get out of jail free' card. I did not get out of my sinful living unscathed. The brokenness, pain, confusion, disappointment, and anguish in my life were the direct result of living outside God's plan. He didn't cause these sufferings or punish me with them. They were merely the effects of the sin I willingly participated in, natural consequences—just as you are naturally burned if you foolishly choose to place your hand in an open flame.

The Enemy knows our wounds and weaknesses and plays on these to trip us up in our faith, but God will never let us be tempted beyond what we can handle. 1 Corinthians 10:13 says He will always provide a way of escape, and it's up to us whether we take that way out or give in to temptation. Unfortunately, I often let the desires of my flesh rule, but God did not turn His back on me, nor did He stop loving me or calling me home. He died for the sins of every person who has lived and will ever live. Not one person is beyond redemption. He died for the sins we have done in the past, and those we will commit in the future. Nothing we can do will ever stop Him from loving us. His arms are always open, calling us to repentance.

On that life-changing night when I encountered God, years of weight and confusion lifted from my mind and were replaced by a sense of love and hope.

He loves me. I am forgiven. I am enough.

As I basked in God's presence and love throughout that moonlit night, He told me to begin writing again, to tell my life story. The book you are now holding is a result of my obedience to His instruction.

Being an author was a childhood dream. Even before I could write I dictated my stories to Dad and he wrote them down for me. This dream was shelved for many years due to the busyness of life. However, when the years of pain, heartbreak, struggle and exhaustion eventually led to a mental breakdown coinciding with the Covid pandemic lockdown, God knew I then had all the time in the world to pick up my love of writing.

The writing brought back cherished memories. I looked through photos of my early years growing up on our family farm with my loving parents and felt such joy and nostalgia over those memories. I grieved too, not for myself, but for that precious, sweet, innocent little girl in the pictures. That cute little child had no idea of the abuse, pain and heartache that was to come, the trauma that would change her forever.

The little girl in the photos was the real Keren, the Keren I was before all the abuse. God had not created me for a broken heart and shattered dreams.

The process of writing about my life was often painful. It was confronting and traumatic to relive experiences I'd rather not dwell on, but this was part of God's reason for telling me to write my story. I could finally process the torrent of bad memories that have wreaked havoc with my mind and emotions for so many years, and begin to heal. As I remember these events, I am comforted by the fact that I know God was, and always will be, right beside me. He'll never leave me alone. He knows, cares, and understands. He is working behind the scenes even when I cannot see evidence of it.

Life has definitely not panned out the way I'd imagined. I am still unmarried, a single mum, and I still struggle financially and battle health issues. None of these things were part of my childhood dreams. But God is good, and I have three amazing, beautiful daughters and two adorable grandchildren. My heart swells and I feel blessed every time I hear them call me Mum or Mema.

Since that moonlit night with God, I've experienced peace that I've never known before. Even when life continues to throw me curve-balls, I am not swayed. I've made a lot of bad choices, and there's a lot of things I considered leaving out of this book for fear of judgment, but I decided it was imperative to leave it all in so it is honest and real and raw. My prayer is that my story will resonate with people who have experienced similar events and trauma in their own lives. I pray they will know they are not alone, and that there is always hope, even during life's darkest moments.

That beautiful evening with God was a pivotal turning point in my life. For many years I'd felt as if I was merely enduring life, being tossed to and fro by the storms that kept pummelling me, leaving me feeling helpless and demoralised, soaked in pain and sadness. Now I can begin to truly live again, to hope and dream once more. I know that God is right here beside me, and no matter what happens in the future, He's got my back.

As a child, I dreamed of travelling to faraway lands. Those dreams have reawakened, and the knowledge that there's a whole wide world out there waiting to be explored and wonders waiting to be seen, makes me excited to live life to the full. I believe that one day I will travel again and have those adventures I've dreamed of all my life.

I still dream of true love. I haven't given up despite all the heartache. God gave me this deep desire for love and marriage, and I know He has an amazing plan in place to see it fulfilled. But that desire is no longer my sole focus in life. I'm leaving it in God's hands. I'm not desperately searching, and I've turned down many offers of dates because I have set very high standards now. After all the pain I've been through, I'm being very careful with my heart and will never allow myself to lower the bar again. While I wait, God is my comfort and my hope, and my children and grandchildren are my delight.

Being a single mum has been hard work. There have been countless times over the years when I've thought about giving up and ending it all, but my daughters and grandchildren have been my reasons to carry on. These five beautiful humans are my pride and joy. I cannot find the words to express how much I love them.

Janaya, Sanjanah and Ahnaliyah had difficult starts in life but have grown into beautiful young women, and I am so proud of them and everything they have overcome.

Janaya is now twenty-three years old and Mum to my two gorgeous grandchildren. She is such a strong mum, working fulltime. She has experienced her own share of hurt and this breaks my heart, but this is her story to tell, not mine. It's natural for a mum to want to protect her children, and I feel like I failed her. I never wanted her to experience pain. She's doing better now, focusing on herself, providing her babies with a loving home, and making precious family memories. I am happy to say that the prayers I prayed since she was a teenager have been answered, and although we don't see each other often due to living on opposite sides of the island, we do enjoy going out for coffees together and our mother-daughter relationship is back on track. I love her strength and tenacity.

Sanjanah was baptised when she was fifteen, and in 2020 she spent a year in Auckland where she attended Equippers Bible College. She is currently now studying nursing in Wellington. When Sanjanah was little, she filled her room with canvases and pictures of Paris and London and faraway destinations. I always knew she was going to travel one day. Since leaving school she's been to Rarotonga and Sydney, taken a cruise around the islands, lived in Auckland for a year, and spent a week in Queenstown for her twenty-first birthday. When she was very young, she told me she wanted to go bungy jumping. I told her if she still wanted to do it when she was sixteen, I'd take her. I thought she would completely forget about it. I was wrong! For her sixteenth birthday we travelled to Taupo where she bungy jumped. She one-upped that last year when she went skydiving. I love her adventurous and gentle spirit.

Ahnaliyah was also baptised at the age of fifteen. When she was seven, she had a heavenly encounter when she saw an angel. Ever since then I have known that God has a great purpose for her life. She is wise beyond her years. She is so passionate and dedicated to Jesus and to seeing people come to Him. At her school, she runs 'By the Gate', a movement of students who gather at their school gate to pray for the students, staff, community and nation. She prayed for many months for an open door within her school to set up and run a Christian group. Her prayers were finally answered and she now runs 'Revo Hub', where each Thursday during the lunchbreak, girls meet to talk about God, do Bible studies, and share devotions and testimonies. She has even preached in church on a number of occasions. Her entire life is focused on loving and serving God, and loving people. God is going to do powerful things in and through her life. I love her steadfastness and dedication.

Cassius has started school now. He enjoys boxing lessons and playing t-ball. When Janaya was in labour with him we had music playing the entire time (I remember lots of Cook Island songs, DJ Khaled, and worship music). *Hosanna* by Hillsong United was playing as he finally made his grand entrance. He loves music and has amazing natural rhythm. He is always singing and dancing and brings so much joy to everyone who is blessed enough to witness his performances. I love his big heart and his hugs.

Evei is such a happy wee girl with the most adorable laugh, and beautiful smile and dimples. She adores her big brother and follows him everywhere. She loves to colour-in and draw, and has a natural, undeniable talent for art, even at a young age. I love her innocent and joyful spirit.

Since my breakdown I've been forced to slow down a lot. I now work part-time in retail and also part-time for my church as the facilitator of a charity called Revolution Lunches where we provide lunches to children who would otherwise go hungry at schools which don't receive the government funded lunches.

I have been single for almost five years, I haven't been drunk for over four years, and I haven't smoked dope for more than twenty years.

It is time for me to grab hold of the baton and carry on the legacy of faith in the race that my forefathers ran; to be an example for my daughters, my grandchildren, and the generations to come.

I received two encouraging words in 2020. The first was from a person I didn't know who had no knowledge of my story. I met her at a women's event at Equippers Church in Napier. These were her words:

28th August 2020

You've had a lot of disappointments in your life. You've experienced grief that you didn't see coming and you didn't imagine happening. God is saying that that time is going to come to an end very soon. It's time to stop grieving. You have grieved long enough. God is going to bring people into your life, people you haven't met before. Your sorrow is going to turn to joy. Happiness is coming. I see laughter, great laughter, coming into your life. You held onto God through all the hard times. At times you were only just clinging on with one finger, but Jesus was holding onto you. He had an elastic band around you and let you pull away. But He's pulling you back now. You're coming into a new season in God. What's coming next is something you never imagined.

The second came from my friend and mentor, Lilias McMinn-Collard:

24th September 2020

You've had a rough road. Life has thrown many boulders in your path. I see you on a dirt road. There's been holes that you've fallen into, and boulders you've had to struggle and crawl to get over. There's been mud, and some of that mud has stuck. There's a great heaviness in your heart, and there's a lot of very deep sorrow in your heart.

You are so tired. Your spirit is tired, your mind is tired, your body is tired, every ounce of your being is tired because you've had to do it all on your own for so long. There's been a lot of confusion. You've had to figure life out for yourself, and you've often been unsure how to navigate all the boulders and holes in the road. You've strived to keep going, to keep moving forward, to somehow continue to put one foot in front of the other. But God's saying, "Just stand." Don't keep striving to move forward, and don't look back on the rough road you've traversed. Just stand with your back to the past.

I can't see what's in your future, but I can see God's summer rain washing over you, washing you clean, washing off all the mud that has stuck to you along your journey of life. Between the rain which washes you clean I see lots of beautiful butterflies coming and landing on you, and I see sunshine shining on you. So, 'just stand' and let God wash you clean.

This brings us to the end of my book, but it is certainly not the end of my story. Now I will hand the pen to God, the One who knows me infinitely better than I know myself, the One who has been right beside me throughout every single moment of my life, through my highest highs and my lowest lows, the One who saw every tear I cried and whose heart broke for mine. He is my knight in shining armour, the One who pushed through the crowd of users, lifted me in His arms and gave me all the love and care I craved. He knows my heart's desires and gently whispers:

> *"I know what I'm doing. I have it all planned out—*
> *plans to take care of you, not abandon you, plans to*
> *give you the future you hope for."*
>
> Jeremiah 29:11, *The Message*

God ... is able to do far more than we would ever dare to ask or even dream of—infinitely beyond our highest prayers, desires, thoughts or hopes.

Ephesians 3:20, TLB

Author's Note

Do you know Jesus? I'd love to introduce Him to you. My life was transformed when I gave my life to Him. No matter what you've done in your life, no matter what you did last week, no matter what you did last night, He is not angry at you. Some people think He is an angry, vengeful God, but rather He's a loving, forgiving and merciful God. He loves you and He wants a relationship with you.

No one is perfect—every single person has sinned—but God has paid the debt for our sins. He died on the cross and took all the penalties of our sins upon Himself. Even if you were the only person on earth, He still would have died *just for you!* He loves you that much, and nothing you do can ever change that. He died so that you can spend eternity with Him in Heaven. He wants *everyone* to be saved, but it's up to you if you want to accept His free gifts of forgiveness, love, and eternity with Him.

> *If you confess with your mouth "Jesus is Lord,"*
> *and believe in your heart that God raised him*
> *from the dead, you will be saved.*
>
> *Romans 10:9*

If you are ready to confess and turn from your sins and begin a new life with God then I invite you to pray this prayer. These are not 'magic' words. The words themselves are not as important as the conviction with which you pray them.

Dear Jesus,

I confess that You are God. I believe that You rose from the dead. I ask You now to become my God, my Lord and Saviour, and my friend. Please forgive me of all my sins. Thank You for accepting me and welcoming me, just as I am. I give my heart to You.

In Jesus' name, Amen.

If you prayed this prayer, please let me know. You can message me via Facebook at: facebook.com/alifeunimaginedkerenmaas

Appendices

A Letter from my Great-Uncle Goff

My dear family,

It is very much my desire to give you some past history of our forefathers, which would otherwise be lost to you in time to come. I will give you briefly some of the interesting history about them. It was passed on to us by our parents, at times when working in the home or in the fields in Germany.

Our name 'Maas' originated from (a man in) France. It is a pity that the place or town where he lived is unknown to us. However, we do know that it was close to Paris. This man Maas and his wife died, during the terrible time of the revolution in France, under the guillotine. Later on, their son eagerly volunteered and joined Napoleon's army. On the way through Germany, this young man Maas came to know a German girl, whom he loved very much. Her name was Sophie, and she was the only daughter of a water miller. Of course, the army had to move on towards Russia, so the man left. Going through Poland however, he became ill and had to stay behind. Here we can see how God cared for him in a very special way, by sparing him from the terrible experience that the French army went through in Russia. It is true that all things work together for good to them that love God.

When the army, what was left of it, returned from Russia, he re-joined them, but he certainly had not forgotten his girlfriend, Sophie. Her parents had warned her that she could hardly expect her boyfriend Geoffrey Maas to return to Russia, but to their surprise one day he turned up on horseback. When the father saw him, he quickly locked his daughter in the cellar, but this soldier was not so easily put off. He forced the door open and put his girlfriend on the back of the horse. At this stage, her father said, "Since you think so much of each other, you might as well get married!" So together, on horseback, they rode to Bremen and got married. Since Sophie, his wife, was the only daughter in the family, Geoffrey therefore became the owner of that watermill. He proved quite a good miller, despite the disadvantage he must have felt in a strange country, not knowing the language or customs.

When he was getting on in years, he very much longed to go back to his own country, to the place where he was born. He took his son with him and they rode on horseback all the way to France; but when they got to his home town, to their big disappointment they could find no trace of his family and relatives. He took a little soil from his parents' grave and put it in a small jar, requesting that at the time of his death, it be placed on his grave with him.

In later years, it was his son who wrote the very nice letter to his children: 'My Last Words to My Dear Children'. As one can see from this letter, he had been a successful miller and a very God-fearing man.

May the Lord help us to follow the guidelines that your great, great Grandfather has reminded us of. May we do this out of love and gratitude for what the Lord and Saviour has done for us!

—G. W. MAAS
Marton, New Zealand 1979

A Brief Family History

My grandad, Wilhelm Maas, was born in Wollingst, Niedersachsen (Lower Saxony) in Germany in 1922, the youngest of six children.

The 1920's were desperate economic times for Germany. Devastated by a draining defeat in World War I, the Versailles Treaty saddled Germany with the payment of war debt and reparations to the victors of the war. Faced with reparation payments they could not afford, Germany began printing enormous amounts of money, creating a state of super inflation. Millions of marks were worthless, and cartoons of the time depicted people with wheelbarrows full of money unable to buy a loaf of bread. People from all walks of life were forced into bankruptcy, and many committed suicide. Taxes became higher and higher as Germany struggled to meet its reparation payments.

In 1930, my great-grandfather, Wilhelm, and great-grandmother, Hermina, sold their farm and booked fares to London and on to Sydney, Australia. As Hermina locked the door of their home in Germany for the last time, she exclaimed, "And now we leave in faith and trust in God."

Grandad was seven at the time. The wagon was loaded, ready to go, and he could not be found. His older brother, Gottfried, was sent to look for him and found him at the back of the house. "I am just having one last look around," Grandad explained.

The family of eight travelled from Hamburg to Southampton, England, on board the American ship *Republic*. One of the first English words they heard was 'wotchastep'. Much later, they realised they were being told to 'watch your step'.

After arriving in Southampton, the Maas family caught a train to London where, on the 23rd of October 1930, they boarded the *Orford* for the five-and-a-half-week voyage to Sydney.

The equatorial heat was intense. With no air-conditioning on board, conditions on the *Orford* were hot and uncomfortable, and most passengers found space to sleep on the open decks. As the ship neared Sri Lanka, the extremity of the heat caused my great-grandfather to suffer a heart attack; he recovered as the ship moved south toward cooler waters.

It was early December when the *Orford* berthed in Sydney. Unforeseen circumstances meant a change of plan for the Maas family. Instead of settling in Australia, they journeyed on to New Zealand, leaving Sydney on board the *Maunganui* on the 19th of December 1930. The Tasman Sea crossing was rough. They reached Auckland on the 23rd of December and travelled by train to Marton, arriving at six a.m. on Boxing Day. It was here that the Maas family settled and made a home.

* * *

My grandad, Wilhelm Maas, married Margaret Jurgens in April 1945, and in May of the following year they welcomed the first of six children, my dad, Lindsay.

Grandad and Grandma were hard working, devoted and loving parents.

Growing up within a farming family, Dad enjoyed a happy childhood. The children made their own fun on the farm, spending summer holidays playing imaginative games under the pine trees. Dad once made an underground hut that provided his younger siblings with hours of fun and adventure.

As a teenager, Dad developed an interest in go-karts, an enjoyable hobby he shared with cousins and friends. He built his own machine when he was about fifteen, showing an aptitude for all things mechanical. This ability progressed into a talent and ingenuity for developing innovative engineering solutions that made work easier when he farmed his own land years later.

It was not unusual at the time for older children to leave school early and help out on the farm or find local employment to support the family. Dad left at fifteen to work on the farm at harvest-time and during the winter he found work in forestry. He was enterprising and resourceful, bought his first tractor while still a teenager and made extra money mowing hay. This was the start of his business as an agricultural contractor.

Dad was intrigued from an early age by his father's stories about the huge acreage of Australian farms and the different farming techniques used on them. Dad had grown up with these legendary tales and was determined to see this Australian agriculture for himself. So when he was twenty, Dad and his cousin Murray travelled over, spending time in South Australia and Queensland.

One of the most interesting features of Dad's travels—an unexpected yet most attractive one—was a young lady named Kayleen (Kay) Schelberg. He met Kay while working on a farm in Macalister named 'Urara', owned by her father Eric.

Dad's brothers wondered what was going on when he returned home from Australia and promptly designed and built a double seat for his tractor. Kay visited Dad in New Zealand a few months later.

* * *

Mum was born and raised in Australia. She was the youngest of three children of Eric and Isabel Schelberg. She has plenty of stories about her childhood growing up on farms in Queensland with her brother and sister, but there is one in particular I remember well.

Mum biked two miles to school in Macalister. One day she was riding home and saw what she thought was a black, burnt stick in the road. As she came closer, the stick moved. She rubbed her eyes, thinking she was imagining it until she biked over the stick and it came to life with a hiss. She was a couple of hundred metres from home when she realised that burnt stick was a snake and that the reptile was now tangled in her bike tyre. Mum screamed, leapt off her bike and ran home crying. Her parents had a hard time trying to figure out what was wrong and where her bike was.

After attending primary schools in both Mt Tyson and Macalister, Mum boarded at Concordia College in Toowoomba, chosen so she could be confirmed into the Lutheran Church. (Mum and Dad were both raised in the Lutheran Church. In the 1970's, with the encouragement of my great-uncle Ferdie, they joined the Pentecostal Church where they discovered a deeper intimacy with God). Back then, some girls went on to higher education but many left school to help around the home. Mum left school at the age of fourteen.

As a teenager Mum enjoyed going out dancing with one of her girlfriends. It was the emergence of the rock 'n roll era and, reminiscent of the movie *Footloose,* dancing was not something 'good Lutherans' were meant to do. One night she wanted to go dancing but the Head of the Queensland Lutheran Church was staying at their family home. Mum stayed at a friend's house after the dance so that he wouldn't find out she had been out rock 'n roll dancing.

In 1966, the pastor at Mum's church received a letter from two young New Zealand men (cousins Lindsay Maas and Murray Nitschke), enquiring about work on farms in the Macalister area. There was no work but Grandfather said they could stay on their farm because they had been in New Zealand the year before and the people had been so kind to them. (Coincidentally, one of the people the Schelberg family had spent time with while in New Zealand was Murray's sister Nita and her husband David).

Mum was captivated by the very handsome twenty-year-old Lindsay Maas who had only intended to stay at the farm for one week but ended up staying for almost three months.

* * *

Mum and Dad were married the following year on the 22nd of July 1967 at the Lutheran Church in Dalby, Australia. They honeymooned on the Gold Coast, journeyed back to New Zealand aboard the *Angelina Lauro* and settled into life together on a farm outside of Marton.

Their first daughter Melissa was born in 1969, followed by Brigitta in 1971, Ingrid in 1974, and finally me, Keren, in 1980.

The farm on Union Line where my sisters and I were raised was named 'Little Urara' after my grandfather's (Eric Schelberg's) farm in Australia where Mum and Dad first met.

Mum remembers being on a train from Wellington to Marton on the way home from a holiday in Australia visiting her family. "I had always wanted to move back to Australia and we had been looking at farms there," she recalls, "but on the train ride home this particular day I got the strong impression from God that this was the land of milk and honey, and from that moment on all my desires to go back and live in Queensland left me. I was content to be here."

Mum was born again at a Pentecostal outreach in Wanganui in the 1970's. A few days later she was outside doing household duties, cleaning and caring for her three young daughters, while reminiscing on what had transpired at the outreach—it had been so different from anything she had experienced growing up within the Lutheran Church. She happened to glance up and was awed by a supernatural vision in the sky. The words, 'You are saved', were right there written across the sky as confirmation to her that God loved her and that she was indeed redeemed. This miraculous message direct from God filled Mum with an indelible peace and assurance that God was real and she was His child.

It is inspiring to see how my family have loved and honoured God throughout the generations and how, in return, God has shown

Himself to be faithful. I have also seen God's faithfulness interwoven into my own story despite the Enemy's attempts to try and take me out. Like my ancestors, my hope is that my testimony will witness to future generations about the goodness of God.

Testimony of my Father

Lindsay Maas - December 2009

As many of you may know, in August 2009 I was diagnosed with medically incurable prostate cancer. By the time the cancer was discovered it had already spread into my pelvis, spine, ribs and shoulder bones, and the doctors glumly informed us that it was too late for chemotherapy or radiation, and too late to operate. Of course, our initial reaction was one of shock. But we quickly came to the realisation that although medically, the doctors say there is nothing they can do for me, God is the greatest physician, and with Him on our side we had nothing to fear.

> *Yea, though I walk through the valley of the shadow of death, I will fear no evil; for You are with me; Your rod and Your staff, they comfort me.*
>
> *Psalm 23:4, NKJV*

With no medical hope given, Kay and I turned to God, through whom all things are possible.

> *What is impossible with man is possible with God.*
>
> *Luke 18:27*

> *For with God nothing will be impossible.*
>
> *Luke 1:37, NKJV*

We felt, "We don't know what to do, but our eyes are on Him." I am in His hands now and it's been such a wonderful experience. Some may think this is strange, but I truly have an uncanny sense of joy. I am rejoicing in my situation, drunk on the presence of the Spirit of God.

Rejoice in the Lord always. I will say it again: Rejoice! Let your gentleness be evident to all. The Lord is near. Do not be anxious about anything, but in every situation, by prayer and petition, with thanksgiving, present your requests to God. And the peace of God, which transcends all understanding, will guard your hearts and minds in Christ Jesus.

Philippians 4:4-7

I am actually glad that the cancer is medically incurable, because I cannot begin to explain the indescribable sense of peace we have both been experiencing through this time. We feel an overwhelming sense of God's tangible presence enveloping us, and to be completely honest, I'd rather have a terminal illness and be experiencing this indefinable closeness with our Creator, than to be completely healthy and be without the oneness and comfort we have found in Him recently. I want to take this opportunity to thank all the people who have taken the time to pray for me over the past months. I know there are many people praying who do not even know me. This is very humbling, and we are so grateful for the prayers of our extended family in Christ from all around New Zealand and the world.

Pray for each other so that you may be healed. The prayer of a righteous man is powerful and effective.

James 5:16

The earnest (heartfelt, continued) prayer of a righteous man makes tremendous power available (dynamic in its working).

James 5:16, AMP

Over the months since my prognosis, I have experienced no

symptoms of cancer. The doctors have given me numerous boxes of painkillers with the expectation that I would need them, but to this date I have not needed a single one. We are accounting this to the grace and healing power of our Father in Heaven.

He was pierced for our transgressions, he was crushed for our iniquities; the punishment that brought us peace was upon him, and by his wounds we are healed.

Isaiah 53:5

Praise the Lord, my soul, and forget not all his benefits—who forgives all your sins and heals all your diseases.

Psalm 103:2-3

PSA blood tests are a way of monitoring the possibility of the presence of cancer. A normal PSA level would be 4 or 5, and as soon as it gets to 10 then the doctors begin to worry. Over the period of months that I was left waiting for a biopsy, blood tests revealed PSA's climbing from 40 to 50, and then to an astonishing 2000! I am currently undergoing six-monthly anti-androgen injections. Since beginning these treatments, my PSA levels have dropped from 2000 to 400, to 127, and at the time of my last test they're down to 72. Whether this is due to the medical intervention or divine intervention it is hard to say. All I can be sure of is the peace and inexplicable joy that we've found in God. For months, Kay and I have been absolutely intoxicated with the infallible presence of God.

In your presence there is fullness of joy.

Psalm 16:11, NKJV

Surely you have granted him unending blessings and made him glad with the joy of your presence.

Psalm 21:6

Ahnaliyah's Angelic Vision

When Ahnaliyah was seven years old, she saw an angel. The morning after, she wrote the following:

On the 29.3.12 when I was 7 years old, I saw an angel. It was about 2:45 in the morning and I was in Mum's bed. It was going to Sanjanah's bedroom. It had a golden dress and short blonde hair. It was glowing with heaps of light around it, and it was so beautiful. It was floating in the air just above the ground. I think it was a boy but it was a bit hard to tell. I felt very glad that Jesus let me see an angel. Mum was feeling very funny and couldn't sleep for a long time before I saw the angel. I think that Grandad said to God to send an angel so I can see one so that I know they are real. Angels are all around us but we don't always see them. I am very lucky to have seen one. Mum and my sisters have not seen one yet, and I'm younger than them. I think that Jesus will let me see some more things like that as I'm growing up.

Acknowledgements

All honour and glory to You, God. Without You this book would have never come to fruition. Thank You for being beside me throughout every single moment of my life—on the highest mountains, and in the lowest valleys. Thank You for never leaving me. Thank You for exchanging beauty for ashes. Thank You for leading me to write this book and for Your hand over the entire process. I pray this book brings You glory.

Thank you to my writing mentor, Jane Bissell, who helped me to mould my forty years of memories into a readable story. You knew all the right questions to ask to fill any gaps in my narrative. I am eternally grateful for your encouragement, support and advice.

A huge thank you to the wonderful Anya McKee at Torn Curtain Publishing for helping me turn my somewhat disjointed manuscript into a beautiful story that perfectly captures everything I wanted to convey and so much more. I am beyond grateful for you and your Spirit-led guidance, your God-centred work ethic, and your prayers.

Thank you to Jean Tidy of Haven Counselling for walking alongside me throughout the writing process and for helping me to process some of the tougher memories this project dredged up. Thank you for helping me begin to heal from any residual guilt and shame that resurfaced as I wrote.

Thank you to Nick and Lilias McMinn-Collard who believed in me and this project enough to support it financially in the beginning stages. Thank you also to Lilias for being my precious friend and mentor during my darkest moments over the past five years.

Thank you to all those who donated towards the costs of writing and publishing this book.

Thank you to my Marton Assembly of God church family who walked along side me during my first twenty-eight years of life.

Thank you to my Equippers church family for being my 'village' over the past fourteen years.

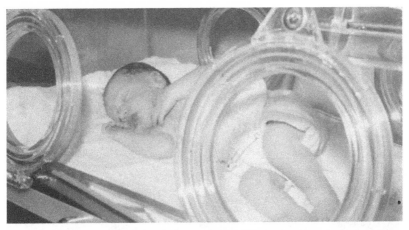

Me at two days old (October 1980)

My big sisters and I

Enjoying life on the farm

A little older, with my sisters

Dad and Mum, my big sisters and I

Dad and I

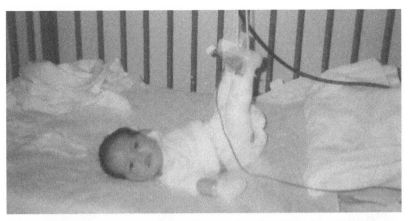

Baby Janaya in hospital with a broken leg (October 1998)

Janaya and Sanjanah (May 2001)

Me during the party years (2001-02)

Janaya, Sanjanah and Ahnaliyah (2004)

The girls and I (2010)

Back: Me, Melissa, Ingrid. Front: Mum, Dad, Brigitta (2010)

A childhood dream came true while Mason and I were holidaying on the Gold Coast, Australia ... swimming with dolphins! (2014)

Monkey Forest (Bali 2015)

From left to right: Ahnaliyah, Sanjanah, me, Janaya (2017)
Photo credit: Marelize White du Plessis

From left to right: Janaya with Evei, George with Cassius, me,
Ahnaliyah and Sanjanah (2019)
Photo credit: Marelize White du Plessis

CPSIA information can be obtained
at www.ICGtesting.com
Printed in the USA
LVHW101935130822
725854LV00001B/83